# THE LITTLE CLAY CART

*SUNY Series in Hindu Literature*
*Edited by Arvind Sharma*

# *The Little Clay Cart*

An English translation of the
*Mṛcchakaṭika* of Śūdraka,
as adapted for the stage
by A. L. Basham

Edited by Arvind Sharma
Introduced by Robert E. Goodwin

STATE UNIVERSITY OF NEW YORK PRESS

Published by
State University of New York Press, Albany



Printed in the United States of America



For information, address State University of New York Press, State University Plaza, Albany, N.Y., 12246

Production by Cathleen Collins
Marketing by Dana Yanulavich

**Library of Congress Cataloging-in-Publication Data**

Śūdraka.
[Mṛcchakaṭika. English]
The little clay cart / an English translation of the Mṛcchakaṭika of Śūdraka, as adapted for the stage / by A. L. Basham; edited by Arvind Sharma; introduced by Robert E. Goodwin.
p. cm. — (SUNY series in Hindu literature)
Includes bibliographical references and index.
ISBN 0-7914-1725-5. — ISBN 0-7914-1726-3 (pbk.)
I. Basham, A. L. (Arthur Llewellyn) II. Sharma, Arvind. III. Title. IV. Series.
PK3798.S91M713 1994
891'.22—dc20 92-46701
CIP

10 9 8 7 6 5 4 3 2 1

*This is the most realistic of Indian dramas, unravelling a complicated story, rich in humour and pathos and crowded with action, of the love of a poor brahman, Cārudatta, for the virtuous courtesan Vasantasenā; this story is interwoven with one of political intrigue, leading up to the overthrow of the wicked king Pālaka, and the play contains a vivid trial scene, after which the hero is saved from execution at the last moment. It is notable for its realistic depiction of city life, and for its host of minor characters, all of whom are drawn with skill and individuality. It has more than once been performed in translation on the European stage, and, to a Western audience, is certainly the most easily appreciated of Indian plays.*

—A. L. Basham, *The Wonder That Was India* (New York: Grove Press, 1954), p. 441

*[The* Mṛcchakaṭika *of King Śūdraka] has been translated repeatedly and adapted for the stage. In Paris it was produced in 1850 and in another adaptation in 1895. In Germany one adaptation of* Mṛcchakaṭika *has attracted large audiences to the theatres about 1892-93 and more recently again—only two or three years ago—another version was produced at Dresden and Leipzig. At the latter place I saw it myself in 1921.*

—M. Winternitz, *Some Problems of Indian Literature* (New Delhi: Munshiram Manoharlal Publishers, 1978), p. 59-60

# *Contents*

# *Preface*

Professor A. L. Basham died on January 27, 1986, in Calcutta. To say that he was the dean of Indologists would be to state the obvious, and to say that his death represented a great loss to the world of Indology would be to succumb to cliché. Fortunately, as one who taught for many years on the same continent as he (though not at the same university) and therefore had opportunities of collegial interaction, my memories are more personal and tinged with emotion. Few who heard his farewell talk at a dinner in Sydney when he left the shores of Australia for good (after retiring from his position as Professor and Head of the Department of Asian Civilization at the Australian National University at Canberra) could remain unmoved, even though as academics we tend professionally to pride ourselves on maintaining a certain distance from the affective domain.

While his colleagues were still coming to terms with his death, I happened to attend the 1986 Annual Conference on South Asia at the University of Wisconsin at Madison. Professors Willard G. Oxtoby and Kenneth G. Zysk also happened to be present. On November 9, 1986, they called to invite me to discuss the matter of the publication of the posthumous papers of A. L. Basham. I felt it a singular honor to be included in these deliberations. Among the papers there was a mimeographed script of the drama *The Little Clay Cart*, about which professors Oxtoby and Zysk wished to ascertain my willingness to prepare it for publication. I was delighted to accept the offer not only on account of the cordial relations I had enjoyed with Professor Basham and the academically congenial nature of the assignment, but also out of the regard I had for Mrs. Namita C. Basham, whom I had had the pleasure of meeting earlier in Australia and more recently during her visit to Canada.

Part of the task assigned to me, apart from preparing the play for publication, was to ascertain as best as I could the circumstances in which the translation came to be made and the play staged. Although I was then in Canada, I was able in this respect to secure the help of Faye Sutherland of the University of New South Wales, Sydney, Australia, who for some years had served on the staff of the Australian Association of Asian Studies. On August 28, 1989, I received from her a letter in which she pieced together, with detective skills worthy of a Sherlock Holmes, the following account of how the play came to be translated into English by Professor Basham and then produced for the stage by Mrs. Joyce Gibson:

> *The Little Clay Cart* was performed by the Hampstead Theatre Club, England in 1964 using a translation by Oliver adapted by Reece Evans. This translation was subsequently published and obtained by Mrs. Joyce (known as Jo) Gibson. Jo Gibson was active in repertory theatre in Canberra, had staged other classical works (Greek) and was on the look-out for likely plays to produce. Knowing Prof. Basham's skills in Sanskrit she took it to him. He was critical of the translation and offered "then and there" to translate it. She said he did this very rapidly and improved on the translation immensely—making it less "flowery" and improving on the colloquial impact of the piece. They collaborated closely with the production, which was staged by the Arts Council of Australia in conjunction with the KALIDASA Society—a society which originated at the ANU to study Indian culture. Prof. Basham supplied most of the music—the Indian High Commission the rest. It was apparently cut down to 2 hrs 30 mins and was produced in a hall on campus on four nights, July 17-20, 1968.

While I was thus engaged in the preparation of the translation of Professor Basham's adaptation of *The Little Clay Cart* for posthumous publication—an adaptation that necessitated its reduction to three-fourths of its original length and some intertextual adjustments and alterations—I attended the 202nd annual meeting of the American Oriental Society at Boston in April 1992. There I heard Professor Robert E. Goodwin present a paper based on the play that delectably spelled out the subtle nuances of literary appreciation its reading involved. I was delighted to hear it and all the more delighted when Professor Goodwin accepted my request to use his paper as the introduction to Professor

Basham's adaptation and translation of *The Little Clay Cart*, as a way of familiarizing readers with the art of appreciating it.

Professor Basham is no longer with us but his fame survives. I hope that the publication of this translation will once again remind us not only of the lasting contribution he made toward rendering Indian culture sympathetically accessible to the West; but also of the fact that, when it comes to scholars, death should not be proud—for, as the Sanskrit poet says, their physical body may perish but the ethereal body of their fame is incorruptible.

# *Introduction*

## Cārudatta in Love, or, How to Appreciate *The Little Clay Cart*

ROBERT E. GOODWIN

The play *Mṛcchakaṭika* or *The Little Clay Cart*, attributed to a certain King Śūdraka, about whom we have no reliable information,[1] has always been praised for its "realism" in a body of literature—not simply drama (*nāṭya*) but all of Sanskrit poetry (*kāvya*)[2]—noted rather for its refined, idealizing, courtly sentiment centering in erotic fascination. We welcome *The Little Clay Cart*'s bourgeois setting and picaresque characters, more typical of the less exalted genre of story literature (*kathā*) than of *kāvya*. Critics likewise praise it for the sweetness of its protagonists, the Brahman merchant Cārudatta and the noble prostitute Vasantasenā, whose love for each other, in the words of S. K. De, is "pure, strong and tender" for all the simplicity of its presentation.[3] Yet this blanket praise, which extends to Śūdraka's "genius" as a constructor of plots and a writer of muscular verse, conceals certain problems. How realistic, for instance, can melodrama be? In what sense can Cārudatta's love be called "strong," even if we were willing to admit that it is "pure and tender?" What was the meaning to a contemporary audience of a play which celebrates the ascendancy of an obscure "man of heart" who never acts in his own behalf, though he spends a remarkable amount of time lamenting his condition? Criticism of the play has to this time hardly scratched the surface.

The principal problem posed by the play is the hero's displacement, and this inevitably involves us in the question of his status as a lover.[4]

Like the hero (*nāyaka*) of every play treating love in a serious way, Cārudatta is a *rasika* ("man of feeling") or *sahṛdaya* ("man of heart")—synonymous terms for the idealized representative of India's classical aesthetic culture. But Cārudatta, an impoverished Brahman merchant, is different from most *sahṛdayas* represented in drama.

First of all, most of them are kings, whose charismatic centrality to the sociopolitical system is taken for granted. Cherished simultaneously as master, friend, childlike protégé, and lover, such a figure's sensibility represents the privilege of power and sets the standard of taste and feeling for the whole society. This situation is apt enough: few would disagree with the idea that India's aesthetic culture radiated out from the courts. But more important as a marginalizing factor than Cārudatta's hybrid social class as such—a Brahman functioning as a Vaiśya[5]—is his poverty. There are other nonroyal *nāyakas*, such as Mādhava of Bhavabhūti's *Mālatīmādhava* (eighth century), who like Cārudatta is a Brahman but nevertheless functions as a typical lovestruck hero (*dhīralalita nāyaka*).[6] We should not forget either that when we speak of Indian court culture we are in fact referring to a hybrid of the courts and the urban elite.[7] But Cārudatta cannot be a Mādhava primarily because he has the not-so-curious idea that beautiful women belong to the world of wealth and power in which he no longer has a share.

Thus, the problem of the hero's displacement hinges on the barrier lack of means creates between the refined *rasika* sensibility and the *nāgarika* life-style that typically goes with it. This in turn implicates love, because erotic feeling (*śṛṅgāra*) is at the very heart of the *rasika* sensibility and indeed of the whole classical Indian aesthetic.[8] What does it mean to be a man of heart or feeling with tastes and inclinations that one cannot afford to indulge? No doubt there were many real-life *sahṛdayas* in Cārudatta's situation, and we would probably not be wrong in seeing this play as speaking directly to their concerns—and incidentally providing them with a wish-fulfillment conclusion.

Let us look first at Cārudatta's credentials as a *sahṛdaya*. We see from his appreciative remarks on music at the beginning of Act 3 (stanzas 3-5) that he has command over the technical vocabulary of connoisseurship, but, more important, that he has the *sahṛdaya*'s imaginative capacity, as when he praises the lute as "companion to the longing lover's heart" and "the delight that increases the passion of the impassioned" and hears in the singer's voice the hidden presence of a beautiful woman.

He thus exhibits that subtly erotic sensibility that Ānandavardhana sees as the lifeblood of the "poetic universe" (see note 8). Cārudatta also has clear—if erotically muted—links with the *nāgarika* as described in *Kāmasūtra* 1.4: I am thinking especially of the litter of musical instruments that makes the Brahman thief Śarvilaka think he has broken into the house of a dance teacher (3.18+). But more important than these more or less technical recommendations is Cārudatta's tenderheartedness (*sānukrośatva, hṛdayasaṃvāda*). All *sahṛdaya* heroes and heroines have this quality to a marked degree, as when Udayana, the royal protagonist of Bhāsa's *Svapnavāsavadatta* (*Vision of Vāsavadattā*), refuses to disturb a bough on which male and female bees may be enjoying love. The princess Padmāvatī in the same play falls in love with Udayana simply by hearing an account of his agonies upon the supposed death of his wife Vāsavadattā. Tenderheartedness is thus a sympathy that unites all exemplary "persons of heart" in a self-conscious community of feeling. Cārudatta has this to an exceptional degree; indeed, we know from several passages that he has lost his father's fortune by lavishing wealth on those who have provoked his sympathetic response, and throughout the play we see ample evidence of his generosity even with the little he has.

The point of this review is to see that the aesthetic, erotic, social, and ethical features of "being a person of heart" (*sahṛdayatva*) are all part of one emotional complex. The last item—the ethical perspective—is of special import in *The Little Clay Cart*. Much is made of Cārudatta's "virtue" or "merit" (*guṇa*) in this play. But when we examine this concept we see that it is in fact a synonym for sympathetic generosity, that is, acting on the basis of "concord of heart" (*hṛdayasaṃvāda*)—what in aesthetic terms is the basis of *rasa*-feeling.[9] In other words, here we have a concept of *dharma* (moral duty) that has little to do with ritualistic obedience to caste norms and such (*svadharma*), but rather represents an aesthetic-sentimental ideal parlayed into a utopian ethical principle. If everyone were like Cārudatta—if everyone acted upon the impulses of a refined and generous sensibility—then *dharma* would mean the satisfaction of the heart's desire for love, friendship, and an honored place in a world that set the truth of inner goodness over words and appearances. The ending of the play is utopian in just this sense: Cārudatta is made a prince, Vasantasenā is released from prostitution, a fugitive becomes king, a former thief becomes a minister, and so on. All men of heart emerge from the obscurity where they had been marginalized by a ruling class that cared only for money, power, and luxury, to inaugurate a new world order based on respect for the sentimentalized concept of virtue as sympathetic generosity (*guṇa* as *sahṛdayatva*). Cārudatta even extends his generosity to his former tormentor, the Śakāra, the previous king's brother-in-law and a grotesque parody of what it is to be a *nāgarika* without the inner sensibility that makes for true aesthetic taste and courtly erotism.

The mention of the Śakāra brings us back to the question of Cārudatta's character as a lover. Here we encounter a fundamental paradox. The logic of the play demands that we think of Vasantasenā as the ideal beloved (*nāyikā*) of Cārudatta. She is the beautiful woman not of the court who in the corrupt world order can only function as a prostitute, and whose *dharma*, we are reminded in the play (1.31-32), is to give herself to whoever can afford her. But beneath the veneer of appearances she is as true a heart as Cārudatta himself, praised by those who know as the virtual goddess of the city (1.27, 1.55+, 5.12, 6.14, 8.39). Thus we would expect Cārudatta, who in fact shares this view, to act upon it or at least to pine for her secretly. And to a limited extent he does. When accident takes her to his house in Act 1 he remarks to himself:

> Ah, it is Vasantasenā—
> The desire inspired by whom has, with the end of my wealth,
> Subsided within my body like the anger of a coward.[10]

Such words would seen to indicate that he has longed for Vasantasenā even since he met her in the garden of the Love-god's shrine, as she has for him (e.g., 1.32+). But Cārudatta can never make up his mind which Vasantasenā he believes in—the fellow *sahṛdayā* or the venal prostitute who belongs to the power structure from which he is barred. To wit, the ninth verse of the fifth act:

> The man who has money will be her lover
> for she can be won with wealth.
> (No, she can be won with virtues!)
> As wealth has abandoned us,
> so she will abandon me.[11]

Thus Cārudatta as a lover is a great puzzle. Returning to the verse cited above ("Ah, it is Vasantasenā . . ."), we can say only that this is a very tepid response for any hero of Sanskrit drama who has been pining for his dream woman. Externally his speech is elegant and deferential: disgusted by the Śakāra's pursuit of her he calls her rather a "women fit to be worshipped as a goddess" (*devatopasthānayogyā yuvatir iyam*), and Vasantasenā is sufficiently impressed by signs of his urbanity (*nāgarikatva*) to plan a strategy for seeing him again. But when he walks her home at the end of Act 1 he recites a verse on the moon that seems to raise erotic expectations only to dash them with a comic ineptitude worthy of his rival the Śakāra:

> Behold the rising moon, pale as a lovely woman's cheek,
> beacon of the highway, with his retinue of stars,
> whose bright rays fall amidst the darkness
> like streams of milk in liquid mud.[12]

And this is the way it goes throughout the play, with only one significant exception, which I will describe in a moment, in Act 5. Although we have ample evidence of Vasantasenā's pining for Cārudatta (absorption in a love-portrait, inconsequential conversation, virtual death with his name on her lips, etc.), there is not one direct indication in the play of his pining for her. In the scene mentioned earlier in which, walking home at night from a concert, he reveals a sensitivity to music's erotic overtones, one would expect this sensitivity to lead, as it would for any other love-hero in such a situation, to some recollection of Vasantasenā's beauty—but it never comes. He falls into an easy sleep a short time later, having thought of her only in connection with his promise to guard her ornaments. In fact his reference to her in this regard is hardly flattering: he wants the Vidūṣaka to keep the jewels out of the inner quarters because "they have been worn by a public woman" (*prakāśanārīdhṛta eṣa*, 3.7).[13] In Act 7, though Cārudatta ostensibly waits for Vasantasenā's arrival in an abandoned garden at the edge of town (a situation fraught with potential for poetic expressions of longing), he never spares a thought for her, even before he meets the future King Āryaka who arrives in the coach that was supposed to carry her. In acts 9 and 10, when he is, respectively, on trial for murdering her and on the way to execution, his thoughts concerning her (with one formulaic exception) have nothing to do with her own plight but rather with the ignominy that has fallen on himself in being accused of murder and theft.[14] Cārudatta is an extremely self-absorbed lover—not in the sense that he loses interest in the mundane world that surrounds him, as other love-heroes do, but in the sense that he can only think of his own misery, society's apparent disregard and contempt of him.

Yet there is the blip in Act 5: Vasantasenā comes to his house as an *abhisārikā*[15] and teases and cajoles him into making love with her. It is hard to avoid the impression of a certain maternal solicitation in this scene: a beautiful woman wise in the ways of the world doting on a bashful adolescent. But, surprisingly enough, Cārudatta rises to the challenge with the aplomb of an inveterate man of feeling (*rasika*), delivering several erotic (*śṛṅgāra*) verses on the torture of his lonely vigils, the ecstasy of her touch, the excitatory stimulus of the rains, and so on. We should not downplay this scene, because it does reveal Cārudatta's *rasika* soul in the classical pattern; yet we cannot help seeing it as something of an irregularity in this play. It establishes Cārudatta's credentials as a bona fide *sahṛdaya*, alive to the quasi-mystical satisfactions of erotic thrill, but it does not tip the scales in the direction of erotic love as a rapturous transcendence of mundanity as opposed to sentiment as an ethical principle.

To see this in all its clarity we have to move to the climactic moment in Act 10 when Vasantasenā virtually rises from the dead to save him. Just before she arrives, while he is still in the depths of despair, he invokes her in heaven to bear witness to his innocence:

> If *dharma* still prevails for me,
> ruined by Fortune through the lies of the powerful,
> may she herself, in Indra's world or elsewhere,
> remove my crime by her own true being.[16]

The structural opposition expressed here is between true being (*svabhāva*) and virtue (*guṇa*) on the one hand and false speech (*vākya*) and wealth-and-power (*dhana, artha*) on the other. Cārudatta has so little confidence in his own speech as to have allowed himself to subscribe to the confession that his enemy has put into his mouth. But whereas before this he has always tended to include Vasantasenā among those who live in and for the world of appearances, now he explicitly includes her in the circle of mute, inglorious *sahṛdayas* who constitute the inner substance, the *svabhāva*, of society. If *dharma* is a matter of *svabhāva* rather than *vākya*, then somehow a miracle will happen and Vasantasenā will penetrate the tissue of corrupt social discourse with the hidden truth. And, of course, this is precisely what happens. She arrives in the nick of time: he describes her in two apt similes, like "rain to a withering crop" and "saving knowledge to a dying man."[17]

Thus we must evaluate the significance of love in this play in the socioethical context we have described. The issue here is not momentary transcendence in an aesthetic-erotic bliss and its problematic consequences, as we find in other plays (e.g., Kālidāsa's *Śakuntalā*). Rather, the accent is on love as the most concrete instance of *sahṛdaya* solidarity. Love is the *svabhāva*, the true being, that triumphs over deceptions. As Cārudatta says to his savioress:

> You yourself have redeemed the body
> that was being destroyed because of you.
> How powerful is the lovers' union,
> when even the dead come back to life![18]

For the *sahṛdaya* on the margins of wealth and power, true feeling (*rasa*) is both more and less than a rapturous shiver of delight. It is the ticket to utopia that the proprietors of the beautiful have corrupted by setting a price on it, that is, by making it a matter of style rather than substance.[19]

That Vasantasenā be the pursuer rather than the pursued in this love affair is, then, of critical importance for two reasons. Cārudatta is a symbol of the *sahṛdaya*'s essential purity, which in this context means a free-floating emotional sympathy devoid (at least ostensibly) of self-interest. Taking a hint from the vaguely Buddhist atmosphere of the play, we might refer to him as a secular Bodhisattva, interested in everyone's salvation but his own. Such a function does not sit well with erotic infatuation, which removes lovers emotionally or psychologically from society into a charmed private sphere. Nevertheless, erotic feeling (*śṛṅgāra*) is too important to the *rasika* sensibility for it to be altogether absent. Thus it is given a certain scope to appear in its customary dimensions, but beyond that it is sublimated as a form of devotion to goodness (*guṇa*), not essentially different from—and on the whole inferior to—the all-male friendship bond.[20]

The second reason is closely related to the first. Vasantasenā is one of several figures in the play who are implicated in the old order but change sides. A good example is the guard Candanaka, who lets Cārudatta's coach pass with Āryaka safely inside. All of these people choose to follow the dictates of the heart to their own practical disadvantage, and all do so with a direct reference either to Cārudatta or to the affective idea of virtue that he epitomizes.[21] Seen in this light Vasantasenā's choice of Cārudatta despite his poverty and her rejection of wealthy but insensitive clients is an act of self-redemption. Thus, her "death" at the hands of the Śakāra symbolizes her complete severance of ties with the world of venal prostitution,[22] and her recovery—aided by the Buddhist monk whom she had earlier helped in Cārudatta's name—is her decisive rebirth into the value-world of sympathetic generosity (*hṛdayasaṃvāda*). Cārudatta, we remember, was never able to decide who the real Vasantasenā was. This is because the burden of the decision has been entirely upon her shoulders. Cārudatta remains what he is throughout the play, the lodestar of virtue by which others guide their actions. His generosity to Āryaka, his fellow victim, is less a defining moral choice than another instance of his essential character (*svabhāva*).[23] It is for others to make such a choice, and in so doing they choose Cārudatta, the unsung hero of society,[24] or his proxy Āryaka, who regards him as the patron saint of the utopian order ushered in by the successful revolution.[25]

But we cannot end this introduction without reverting to the play's incidental function as wish fulfillment. For all the ideality of his character we have no trouble seeing that Cārudatta himself is not really free of the idea that wealth and virtue are closely related. He spends an inordinate amount of time brooding on his poverty, with its concomitant loss of friends and reputation. Yet why should one who represents true being (*svabhāva*) over appearance (*vākya*) be so concerned with the judgment of superficial people? How, furthermore, can he be so blind to the general esteem in which he is held among all persons of heart? He is never so ashamed as when he cannot display his generosity in material terms. Thus, when he has to let the good news whispered into his ear by Vasantasenā's maid go unrewarded, it launches a series of verses on the theme of impotence:

Oh misery!

For a man without money what is the use
of living in this world at all?
In his inability to reciprocate
both his anger and favor are vain.

Furthermore—

A wingless bird, a withered tree, a waterless pond,
a toothless serpent: a poor man in the human world.

Furthermore—

Poor men are like uninhabited houses,
waterless wells, withered trees,
for, forgetting their woes in union with a friend,
their moments of pleasure thus prove empty.[26]

Again, at that point in Act 3 when his wife provides him with the means of compensating Vasantasenā extravagantly for the loss of her jewels, his first reaction is extreme embarrassment:

What, my wife pities me! Alas! Now I am poor—

My wealth destroyed by a personal fate
and pitied with a woman's wealth:
through wealth a man becomes a woman,
and a woman a man through wealth.[27]

If we put all these hints together we emerge with the portrait of a man who sees generosity as a sort of sexual potency and a claim on the general admiration of society. Cārudatta is not vulgar, like the Śakāra and the corrupt ruling class the latter represents. There can be no questioning the sensibility that makes this meek, displaced hero a genuine *sahṛdaya*. But at the same time there is a psychological dimension that we cannot ignore. Cārudatta's version of potency is based on money, not as a means of directly purchasing aesthetic-erotic satisfactions but as a means of inspiring others to love him and act on his behalf. For this reason—and because his very desire for potency is surreptitious—he is essentially passive. It is no accident that when, in the scene mentioned above, Cārudatta reaches for a ring to reward Vasantasenā's maid and then shows embarrassment, Vasantasenā responds, "This is why I love you!" (*ata eva kāmyase*), words that almost exactly echo her earlier response when the Vidūṣaka arrived at the brothel with the gift of Cārudatta's wife's heirloom (4.32+). The very manifestation of what he himself feels as impotence wears a charm that borrows power from the admiring beholder. Cārudatta's gestures have, directly or indirectly, the same effect on all noble souls, who rally to his cause, rescue him from his good-hearted passivity, and make him the prince he was always meant to be.[28] Thus the utopian order based on sympathetic generosity corresponds exactly with the acknowledgment and empowerment of the *sahṛdaya*, the secular Bodhisattva who, like fairy-tale heroes everywhere, gets the girl and the kingdom too.

## NOTES

1. He is first mentioned as an author by the poetician Vāmana (fl. A.D. 800). For further information see Appendix I: The Author. It should be made clear here that this essay is based on the full play. The numbers refer to act and verse according to the readily available edition-translation of M. R. Kale (Delhi: Motilal Banarsidass, 1972).

2. Generically, *kāvya* includes *nāṭya* as one of its two principal forms—the other is *mahākāvya*, sometimes translated as "court epic."

3. S. N. Dasgupta and S. K. De, *A History of Sanskrit Literature* (University of Calcutta, 1975), p. 245.

4. I am bracketing problems of textual accretion, authorship, and where the play stands in relation to the fragment in the Bhāsa corpus called *Daridra-cārudatta* or *Cārudatta in Poverty*. Like most scholars I regard Śūdraka's play as an elaboration of Bhāsa's. Śūdraka's dependence on the Bhāsa play was established by Georg Morgenstierne, *Über das Verhältnis zwischen Cārudatta und Mṛcchakaṭika* (Halle, 1920), though some have contested it, most recently G. H. Schokker, "Śūdraka, the Author of the Original Cārudatta," in *Pratidānam: Indian, Iranian and Indo-European Studies Presented to F. B. J. Kuiper*, ed. J. C. Heesterman et al. (The Hague: Mouton, 1968). See A. D. Pusalkar, *Bhāsa: A Study*, 2nd ed. (Delhi: Munshiram Manoharlal, 1968) for further bibliography. Also see Appendix II: The Play.

5. In the classical schema the four classes (*varṇas*) are (1) Brahman (priest), (2) Kṣatriya (warrior prince), (3) Vaiśya (farmer, merchant, etc.), and (4) Śūdra (menial and servile occupations). Brahmans have the theoretical lock on society's intellectual function, while Kṣatriyas protect it by force, Vaiśyas provide its material sustenance, and Śūdras perform the services.

6. *The Little Clay Cart* and *Mālatīmādhava* are the two prime examples in the extant literature of a type of play known as the *prakaraṇa*. The requirements of this subgenre are basically that the plot be invented or borrowed from popular stories (*kathā*) as opposed to history and legend (*itihāsapurāṇa*), and that the hero (*nāyaka*) be other than a king, typically a Brahman, a merchant, or a minister. The heroes of Sanskrit drama are divided into four basic types—exalted (*dhīrodātta*), amorous (*dhīralalita*), serene (*dhīrapraśānta*), and vehement (*dhiroddhata*). According to most sources the hero of a *prakaraṇa* must be serene. Although not entirely artificial, these distinctions (1) are mainly *ex post facto*, (2) cannot be made to fit certain obvious cases, and (3) belie the fact that most *nāyakas* are composite types.

7. Thus the greatest of Sanskrit playwrights, Kālidāsa (probably fifth century

A.D.), can have one of his characters call the royal hero of the *Vikramorvaśīya* a *nāgarika* ("urbane townsman") in order to explain his sophistication (*dākṣiṇya*) as a lover (3.13+). It was the *nāgarika* for whom the *Kāmasūtra*, Vātsyāyana's celebrated treatise on erotics (third century?), was written. *Kāmasūtra* 1.4 describes the ideal day of the *nāgarika*, which was devoted entirely to refined amusements and capped by amorous sport. It tells us of *nāgarikas* who joined in *goṣṭhīs* (literary "clubs"), enjoying cultivated conversation with hetaeras, music, poetry, jaunts to the countryside, and so on. Such *goṣṭhīs*, or individual *nāgarikas*, provided important patronage for the arts including troops of actors. In *The Little Clay Cart* Cārudatta's friend Rebhila entertains the members of his *goṣṭhī* with a concert. There is incidentally a whole subgenre of drama devoted to the amorous exploits of the *nāgarika*: the *bhāṇa* or "monologue play." Unfortunately it has not received its share of serious study.

8. Cf. the well-known lines of the poetician Ānandavardhana (ninth century):

> In the boundless world of poetry the poet is the sole creator,
> and as it pleases him, so does the world appear.
> If he has erotic feeling, that world is full of sentiment;
> if he is passionless, it is entirely devoid of feeling.
>
> (*apāre kāvyasamsāre kavir ekaḥ prajāpatiḥ/*
> *yathāsmai rocate viśvaṃ tathedaṃ parivartate//*
> *śṛṅgārī cet kaviḥ kāvye jātaṃ rasamayaṃ jagat/*
> *sa eva vītarāgaś cen nīrasaṃ sarvam eva tat//*)
> —*Dhvanyāloka* 3.42

"Sentiment" or "feeling" (*rasa*), borrowed initially from drama, is the key concept in the Indian theory of poetics from Ānandavardhana on. The *Nāṭya-śāstra*, the most important and earliest Indian treatise on dramatics (compiled over a long period from at least the fifth century B.C. to the third or fourth centuries A.D.), states categorically that "no purpose is achieved without sentiment" (*na hi rasād ṛte kaścid arthaḥ pravartate*).

9. Cf. the celebrated definition of Abhinavagupta in his commentary on Ānandavardhana's *Dhvanyāloka* 1.1:

> *Sahṛdayas* are those who share in a concordance of heart, i.e., who have an aptitude for identification with what is depicted [by poets] in a mirror-like mind made clear by familiarity with the practice of poetry. (*yeṣāṃ kāvyānuśīlanābhyāsavaśād viśadībhūte manomukure varṇanīyatanmayībhavanayogyatā te hṛdayasaṃvādabhājaḥ sahṛdayāḥ*).

10. 1.55:

> *aye iyaṃ vasantasenā/*

*yayā me janitaḥ kāmaḥ kṣīṇe vibhavavistare/*
*krodhaḥ kupuruṣasyeva svagātreṣveva sīdati//*

11. 5.9:

*yasyārthas tasya sā kāntā dhanahāryo hyasau janaḥ/*
*(na guṇahāryo hyasau janaḥ)*
*vayam arthaiḥ parityaktāḥ nanu tyaktaiva sā mayā//*

12. 1.57:

*paśya—*
*udayati hi śaśāṅkaḥ kāminīgaṇḍapāṇḍur*
*grahagaṇaparivāro rājamārgapradīpaḥ/*
*timiranikaramadhye raśmayo yasya gaurāḥ*
*srutajala iva paṅke kṣīradhārāḥ patanti//*

13. It has been suggested that Cārudatta's status as an exemplary householder (*gṛhastha*) explains his apparent lack of erotic interest in the heroine: it would not be "appropriate" for such a hero to pine for a courtesan. There is much to this, yet surely the playwright would have been deft enough to infuse a little more eros into his hero (one or two pining soliloquies), if that had been his interest, without damaging our respect for him. After all, if propriety is the deciding factor, why not avoid the love of Brahman and courtesan altogether?

14. The exception is 10.13, repeated after 10.24 and 10.36, according to stage directions:

O woman with teeth white as pure moonbeams
and lower lip red as coral,
after drinking the nectar of your mouth
must I now drink the poison of infamy?
(*śaśivimalamayūkhaśubhradanti*
*suruciravidrumasaṃnibhādharauṣṭhi/*
*tava vadanabhavāmṛtaṃ nipīya katham avaśo hyayaśoviṣaṃ pibāmi//*)

But even this, though it does raise the specter of her erotic charm, ends in the familiar refrain of self-lamentation.

15. A "woman who goes (to her lover)," one of eight types of heroine (*nāyikā*) classified according to her disposition to her lover.

16. 10.34:

*prabhavati yadi dharmo dūṣitasyāpi me'dya*
*prabalapuruṣavākyair bhāgyadoṣāt kathaṃ cit/*
*surapatibhavanasthā yatra tatra sthitā vā*
*vyapanayatu kalaṅkaṃ svasvabhāvena saiva//*

17. 10:39 and 42:

    Who is this who has come to me
    like rain to a withering crop,
    when the sword was poised
    and I was in the jaws of death?
    (*keyam abhyudyate śastre mṛtyuvaktragate mayi/*
    *anāvṛṣṭihate sasye droṇavṛṣṭir ivāgatā//*)
    Whence have you come
    with tear-soaked breasts
    like saving knowledge
    to this dying man?
    (*kuto bāṣpāmbudhārābhiḥ snāpayantī payodharau/*
    *mayi mṛtyuvaśaṃ prāpte vidyeva samupāgatā//*)

18. 10.43:

    *tvadartham etad vinipātyamānaṃ*
    *dehaṃ tvayaiva parimocitaṃ me/*
    *aho prabhāvaḥ priyasaṃgamasya*
    *mṛto'pi ko nāma punar dhriyeta//*

19. By pertinent analogy, one of the main issues of Sanskrit poetics is the distinction made between genuine poetry, which is suggestive and principally concerned with *rasa,* and pseudo-poetry, which does not get beyond rhetorical sport. Ānandavardhana calls all such poetry *citrakāvya* ("picture poetry"), alluding to poems whose syllables placed in certain arrangements form a schematic wheel or the like. The only criterion of true poetry is that it please the man of heart. See Ānandavardhana, *Dhvanyāloka* 1.1, 1.13, 3.41-42.

20. Note the terms in which the Brahman thief Śarvilaka makes his decision before exiting in Act 4 (4.25):

    Two things—friend and woman—
    are dear to men in this world,
    but now I would choose my friend
    over a hundred beautiful women.
    (*dvayam idam atīva loke priyaṃ narāṇāṃ suhṛc ca vanitā ca/*
    *samprati tu sundarīṇāṃ śatād api suhṛd viśiṣṭatamaḥ//*)

    He has willingly sacrificed his reputation as a Brahman out of love for Madanikā, Vasantasenā's servant, yet no sooner does he win her than he gives her up because his friend Āryaka is in trouble. It is no accident, either, that he more than regains his social status as a result.

21. It might be helpful to refer here to the four "human goals" (*puruṣārthas*) under which rubric all human behavior can be classified in the Hindu

worldview: *dharma* (law, duty), *artha* (profit), *kāma* (desire, pleasure), and *mokṣa* (salvation). Under the old regime *dharma* is confused with *artha:* for example, it is Candanaka's "duty" to arrest the fugitive Āryaka, just as it is Vasantasenā's duty to surrender to the Śakāra, though both of these actions would really be only self-serving. But in the new order *dharma* will be aligned primarily with *kāma*, with the latter understood altruistically as sympathetic generosity (*hṛdayasaṃvāda*), though eventually *artha* follows suit, that is, once the revolution succeeds. How different is this notion of *dharma* for the model of *karmayoga* ("the discipline of action") in the *Bhagavad Gītā*, where the ideal is disinterested ritualistic performance of prescribed duty in the spirit of renunciation regardless of the heart's inclinations. Such a notion of *dharma* would offer no hope for Vasantasenā and the other *sahṛdayas* except in the ultimate sense of *mokṣa.* The affective model of *dharma* in this play is distinctly antinomian, because it offers the possibility of a more fluid social structure than the caste system.

22. Lest we dismiss this aspect of Vasantasenā as mere facade we should recall the Vidūṣaka's carnivalesque description of brothel decadence in Act 4. Even if this scene is an accretion it has hermeneutical value as an indication of the way the indigenous tradition understood the issue at point. Vasantasenā is by implication a queen who presides over a realm of emasculating decadence.

23. Āryaka is Cārudatta's active double, the revolutionary his sympathetic generosity does not allow him to be. By contrast the Śakāra is his "shadow" or "evil twin," absorbing all of Cārudatta's potential sexual aggressiveness, so that his love can be "pure" and "tender" (in S. K. De's terminology). Any anger Cārudatta might feel toward courtesans, who sell their beauty to the highest bidder rather than award it to those with the sensitivity to appreciate it, is transferred to the Śakāra.

24. See the references to his role as 'wishing-tree' (*kalpavṛkṣa*): 1.48, 9.30+, 10.30+ (cf. 2.15+. 4.32, 6.13-14, 10.4).

25. 10.52+: "Good sir, King Āryaka proclaims: 'I have acquired this kingdom by your goodness. Therefore receive [the principate I confer upon you].'" (*ārya nanvayam āryako rājā vijñāpayati—idaṃ mayā yuṣmadguṇopārjitaṃ rājyam/ tad upayujyatām/*)

26. 5.40-42:

*bhoḥ kaṣṭam*
*dhanair viyuktasya narasya loke kiṃ jīvitenādita eva tāvat/*
*yasya pratīkaranirarthakatvāt kopaprasādā viphalībhavanti//*
*api ca/*

*pakṣavikalaś ca pakṣī śuṣkaś ca taruḥ saraś ca jalahīnam/*
*sarpaś coddhṛtadaṃṣṭras tulyaṃ loke daridraś ca//*
*api ca*
*śūnyair gṛhaiḥ khalu samaḥ puruṣo daridraḥ*
*kūpaiś ca toyarahitais tarubhiś ca śīrṇaiḥ/*
*yad dṛṣṭapūrvajanasaṃgamavismṛtānām*
*evaṃ bhavanti viphalāḥ paritoṣakālāḥ//*

27. 3:27:

*kathaṃ brāhmaṇī mām anukampate/ kaṣṭam/ idānīm asmi daridraḥ/*
*ātmabhāgyakṣatadravyaḥ strīdravyenānukampitaḥ/*
*arthataḥ puruṣo nārī yā nārī sārthataḥ pumān//*

For further expressions of impotence, see 1.55 (cited in note 10) and 5.8.

28. Thus to his composite character of Brahman and Vaiśya he adds the quality of being a Kṣatriya: see note 5.

# *Translator's Note*

The translation of the *Mṛcchakaṭika* that follows was made by the noted Sanskrit scholar and author of *The Wonder That Was India* A. L. Basham, who held the chair of Asian Civilization at the Australian National University. He contributed the following program note when the play was staged:

The Sanskrit theatre flourished for about a thousand years, roughly during the first millennium of the Christian era. It evolved out of earlier mime and folk drama, and developed its own distinctive conventions. The stage had no scenery and few properties, and much use was made of formal gesture language, to indicate the background of the action. Plays were generally performed by professional companies, but as far as can be gathered there were no regular theatres. Performances were sponsored by kings and other wealthy patrons, and the audiences were invited ones. But dramas might be performed in the courts of temples, and these were generally open to the public. The dramatist did not cater entirely for an elite audience; he also considered the plain man who might be moved more by dramatic incidents and farcically comic situations than by fine poetry and subtle psychological touches. Plays were written in mixed prose and verse. The main dialogue was normally in prose, but occasional verses were employed to underline an emotion, to describe a scene, to drive home a moral, or simply to add a witty twist to a comic situation.

*The Little Clay Cart* (*Mṛcchakaṭika*) is the work of a certain Śūdraka, who is said to have been a king, but of whom nothing reliable is known. Internal evidence suggests that it was written in the Gupta period (c. A.D. 300-600), the "Classical" Age of Hindu civilization, and probably early in that period, in the fourth century. Unlike most Sanskrit dramas, the plots of which are based either on heroic or religious legend or on the intrigues of royal courts, this play reflects the ordinary life of bourgeois India, and as such it forms a most valuable historical document. It has a brilliantly devised plot, replete with exciting and comic incident, leading up to a climax as exciting as any in the drama of the world. We may compare Śūdraka with Plautus, Shakespeare, or Ben Johnson, but in some ways we may also see him as a remote precursor of Alfred Hitchcock.

The translation is a free one. The structure and idiom of Sanskrit is such that any attempt to adhere closely to the original results in a literary disaster. The full play would probably last for five or six hours, and the text has been drastically cut. Much dialogue has been abridged, and several incidents have been omitted altogether. The original play has an enormous cast, and to reduce this for practical purposes the parts of one or two minor characters have been combined or grafted on to others. A few slight alterations have been made to make the play more suitable for production on a modern stage, and a number of brief phrases have been added here and there, to explain obscure points and allusions to a "Western" audience. Otherwise an attempt has been made to interpret the lively dialogue of the original in contemporary idiom, while translating Śūdraka's complex Sanskrit stanzas into simple English verse. The costumes are not those of modern India, but have been adapted from those portrayed in the sculpture and painting of the period.

The drama reflects a way of life and a set of values in some ways surprisingly similar to those of the contemporary world and in others very different. We are introduced to a society where class and birth are really important, and where polygamy is socially acceptable. Domestic slavery is widespread, but the slave has his rights in law and is able to buy his freedom. Temporary slavery is a common method of paying off debts. Respectable women in general remain in the background, like Dhūtā, the wife of the hero Cārudatta, but the cultured courtesan is a familiar feature of better-class society, and receives a good deal of respect. This play reflects, like much other Indian literature, the symbiosis of the ascetic and the sensuous, the sacred and the profane, in the Indian mind. On the one hand the hero passionately loves the hetaera who is the heroine; on the other he dutifully follows all the Brahmanic domestic rituals and, in the penultimate scene, is ashamed to admit his love in public because this conflicts with the strict Brahmanic moral code.

The play reflects an urbane society which carries its morals lightly in some particulars, but in others sets very high ethical standards. In the theatres of Greece, Spain, France, and Elizabethan England it is unlikely that Cārudatta would have pardoned his enemy so magnanimously. The only really wicked character is also a ridiculous fool. Perhaps this play is more typical of the moral attitude of its times than many contemporary religious texts. The world is full of misfortune. Even good and generous actions may lead to sorrow and trouble. But for all this, life is well worth living, for the world contains many good and beautiful things and there is much happiness in it. The righteous man may suffer, but in the end he is stronger than the wicked, who is really a fool and who misses the wood for the trees. The man who, like Cārudatta, loves his friends and forgives his enemies, even if he is weak and often makes mistakes, will in the end find his reward in a full and happy life.

# *Synopsis*

Vasantasenā is a famous courtesan of Ujjayinī who falls in love with the Brahman merchant Cārudatta, now impoverished by his own charity by being generous to a fault. The son-in-law of the king, Saṃsthānaka, however, wants her for himself. One dark night Vasantasenā seeks shelter in the home of Cārudatta with Saṃsthānaka in pursuit, and deposits her ornaments with Cārudatta for safekeeping before leaving his house when the coast is clear. Vasantasenā has a maid-servant, Madanikā by name, with whom a Brahman named Śarvilaka has fallen in love. He wants to buy her freedom. To obtain the required money he burgles the house of Cārudatta and steals the ornaments left behind by Vasantasenā for safekeeping. Śarvilaka buys the freedom of Madanikā, Vasantasenā's maidservant, by offering Vasantasenā her own ornaments! In the meantime Cārudatta, mortified by the loss of the ornaments left in his charge, concocts the story that he gambled Vasantasenā's ornaments away rather than admit to their theft, and his loyal wife Dhūtā helps him replace Vasantasenā's lost jewelry with her own.

In the meantime the monsoon has broken and Vasantasenā returns to the house of Cārudatta and spends the night there to avail herself of the romantic opportunity provided by the season. In the morning Vasantasenā finds Cārudatta's son Rohasena crying because he owns only a clay cart. Vasantasenā places her ornaments in his cart and asks him to buy a golden one with them. This incident provides the title of the play. Later in the day Cārudatta and Vasantasenā have an assignation in the park called Puṣpakaraṇḍa but by accident she gets into the chariot of Saṃsthānaka. In the meantime a political prisoner escapes and gets into the cart of Cārudatta. The driver, mistaking the rattle of chains for the tinkling of Vasantasenā's ornaments, drives the vehicle away. The escapee, Āryaka by name, is accosted by two police guards; but one of them, being favorably disposed to the prisoner in flight, causes a commotion, allowing the prisoner to get away. On arriving in the park and after being helped by Cārudatta, the prisoner makes his getaway, full of gratitude for his benefactor Cārudatta.

Meanwhile Vasantasenā has also arrived in the park and is in for a nasty surprise. She runs into the wicked Saṃsthānaka whose vehicle she had mistakenly mounted. She spurns the advances of Saṃsthānaka, who is so enraged by her rejection that he chokes her and leaves her for dead. Fortunately she is saved by Saṃvāhaka, a reformed gambler and former friend of Cārudatta now turned Buddhist monk, who takes her to the monastery and revives her.

In the meantime, at the instigation of Saṃsthānaka Cārudatta is charged with the murder of Vasantasenā and is sentenced to death, despite the missing corpus delicti. But there is a dynastic revolution and the escapee Āryaka becomes king, after doing away with the reigning monarch Pālaka who had imprisoned Āryaka on account of a prophecy that Āryaka would someday be king.

The forces of good triumph over evil not a moment too soon. Cārudatta is discharged; he can have Saṃsthānaka killed for falsely accusing him of murder but practices magnanimity in victory and lets him go. The new king reinstates Cārudatta in a position befitting his virtue and the courtesan is raised to dignity by royal decree. Cārudatta and Vasantasenā get married, and the reader is left wondering about the fate of the long-suffering and virtuous wife.

# The Little Clay Cart

## DRAMATIS PERSONAE

Āryaka, Prisoner who subsequently becomes King of Ujjain.
Candanaka, Police officer.
Cārudatta, The hero, a citizen of Ujjain reduced to poverty from his own generosity but still dignified and gracious.
Cūrṇavṛddha, A friend of Cārudatta.
Darduraka, A gambler.
Dhūtā, Wife of Cārudatta.
Maitreya, Companion of Cārudatta, loyal to him to the end.
Madanikā, Maidservant of Vasantasenā.
Māthura, Runs the gambling den.
Pālaka, King of Ujjain who imprisoned Āryaka and was later killed and replaced by him.
Radanikā, Maidservant of Cārudatta.
Rebhila, A merchant and friend of Cārudatta.
Rohasena, Son of Cārudatta.
Saṃsthānaka, The brother-in-law of the reigning king of Ujjain and the villain.
Saṃvāhaka, Professional masseur, also gambler, who becomes a Buddhist monk.
Śarvilaka, A Brahman in love with the maidservant of Vasantasenā called Madanikā: commits larceny.
Sthāvaraka, A servant of Saṃsthānaka.
Vardhamānaka, A servant of Cārudatta.
Vasantasenā, Heroine of the play who is in love with Cārudatta.
Vīraka, Police officer.
Viṭa, A friend of Saṃsthānaka, the villain.

## BENEDICTION

An Introductory Blessing to be recited at the beginning of Act I.

PĀTU VO NĪLAKAṆṬHASYA KAṆṬHAḤ ŚYĀMĀMBUDOPAMAḤ
GAURĪBHUJALATĀ YATRA VIDYULLEKHE 'VA RĀJATE.

May we be guarded by the God Śiva, whose neck is ever embraced by the fair slender arms of the goddess, like pale streaks of lightning flashing upon the surface of a dark blue cloud.*

---

* The PROLOGUE has been omitted by Professor Basham.

# Act I

*Cārudatta's house and streets of Ujjain. Nightfall.*

MAITREYA [*with a cloak over his arm, enters, reading*] "I hope another Brahman invites you, because I'm engaged just now." So I'll have to look for some other invitations. What a mess I'm in. When Cārudatta had money in his pocket I could sit in his courtyard and eat scented sweetmeats day and night if I wanted to. I was like a painter surrounded by his paint pots, dipping into them one after another. If I wanted I could stand in a corner of the market, like a well-fed bull, chewing away without a care in the world. Now he's poor I have to go wherever I can get a meal, but somehow I always come back here, just like a carrier pigeon! Today it's to bring him a present from a friend—this jasmine-scented cloak.

[*Maitreya knocks on Cārudatta's door. The maid Radanikā opens.*]

MAITREYA Is Master Cārudatta at home, my dear?

RADANIKĀ Yes, sir, he's here. He's been praying and he's just going to make an offering to the household gods.

MAITREYA I'll wait till he's finished.

[*Maitreya stands aside. Cārudatta enters and stands in the doorway scattering seed. He sighs and looks upward.*]

CĀRUDATTA Once when I scattered offerings at the door the geese and cranes would fly down after them, they were so plentiful; but now my threshold is all grown up with grass, and only worms eat the few grains I scatter before the gods.

MAITREYA [*going up to him*] Good evening, sir, and good fortune!

CĀRUDATTA So, my old friend Maitreya has come to see me! Welcome Maitreya! Come in!

MAITREYA Thanks, I will. [*Enters.*] Your good friend Cūrṇavṛddha asked me to bring you this cloak. It's scented with jasmine. He says he wants you to wear it when you've finished your prayers.

[*He takes it, still wrapped in his thoughts.*]

CĀRUDATTA
When one knows sorrow, a small joy seems bright as
when one lights a lamp in the pitch darkness. But
he who comes to poverty after comfort is like a
dead man in a living body.

MAITREYA Would you rather have death than poverty then?

CĀRUDATTA
If it comes to a choice between poverty and death
give me death every time, for death is only a
moment's pain, and poverty's endless grief.

It's not that I've grown poor that hurts me so, but rather that old guests avoid my house, now that I've nothing left to give to them.

MAITREYA Those sons of sluts! Put them out of your mind. They're like herd-boys who go wherever the grass is longest!

CĀRUDATTA
It's not so much that I've lost all my money,
that makes me feel unhappy—as fate commands
wealth comes and goes. What burns me up is this—
that when your money's gone your friends all leave you.
Poverty kills one's self-respect; and where
there is no self-respect there's no dignity.
A man without dignity is scorned and slighted;

scorn breeds despair; and from despair comes anguish;
and anguish turns one mad, and madness leads
to utter ruin. So in poverty
is found the root of every human evil.

MAITREYA That's the way it is. Now let's change the subject.

CĀRUDATTA I've made my offerings to the household gods; now you go and sacrifice on my behalf to the Divine Mothers at the crossroads!

MAITREYA [*firmly*] No! I don't want to go!

CĀRUDATTA [*surprised*] Why not?

MAITREYA You've always worshipped the gods and they haven't shown you any favors—so what's the good of worshipping them?

CĀRUDATTA Maitreya, please don't talk like that! To worship the gods is the duty of the head of the house . . . So go and sacrifice to the Mothers.

MAITREYA No, I'm not going! Send somebody else! I always get the ritual wrong anyway, though I'm a Brahman. My mind is like a mirror where left is right and right is left. What's more it's turning dark, and the main roads are full of tarts and loafers and toughs—not to speak of king's hangers-on having a night out! They'd gobble me up like a snake swallowing a mouse! I'm stopping here with you!

CĀRUDATTA All right then, stay here while I go and finish my prayers. [*Exit.*]

VOICES OFF Stop Vasantasenā, stop!

[*Enter Vasantasenā pursued by Saṃsthānaka (the king's brother-in-law) and Viṭa* (his hanger-on) and a slave.*]

VIṬA Wait Vasantasenā! Stop!! Stop!!!

* *Viṭa* is not strictly a proper name, and means a boon companion.

Why let your fear get the better of good breeding,
hurrying along on feet more used to dancing?
Why do you run like a hunted antelope
casting back frightened glances at the huntsmen?

SAṂSTHĀNAKA Stop, Vasantasenā! Stop!!

Why do you run away, tripping as you go?
Wait now, calm down, nobody's going to kill you.
My tortured heart is burning up with love,
like a slice of meat that's broiling on the charcoal.

THE SLAVE Stop, Lady! Stop!!

Why do you run away from us in fear
like a fine peacock in rich summer plumage?
The Lord my Master can run even faster
like a hound chasing a bird in the woods.

SAṂSTHĀNAKA I called her by so many loving names,
such as the Love-God's whip, eater of dried fish,
wanton, flat-nose, the ruin of noble houses,
casket of passions, nymphomaniac,
procuress, heap of finery, prostitute, whore.
All this I've called her—and still she runs from me!

VIṬA You're only a lute plucked by the hands of idlers;
so why do you run away, frantic with fear,
your soft cheeks struck by your earrings, like a heron,
caught in a storm and frightened by the thunder?

SAṂSTHĀNAKA As hounds pursue a vixen through the woods
we give you chase, and yet you run so fast,
so quick, so speedily; and you take away
my heart, with all its veins and arteries!

VASANTASENĀ Pallavaka! Pallavaka! Parabhṛtikā! Parabhṛtikā!!

SAṂSTHĀNAKA Viṭa, Viṭa! There are men coming!

VIṬA It's all right, there's nothing to fear!

VASANTASENĀ Mādhavikā! Mādhavikā!!

VIṬA You idiot, she's only calling her maids.

SAMSTHĀNAKA Is she calling a woman, then?

VIṬA Of course she is.

SAMSTHĀNAKA Women, eh? Who's afraid? I could kill a hundred women with one blow.

VASANTASENĀ Oh dear, all the servants have run away! Now I shall have to look after myself!

SAMSTHĀNAKA Vasantasenā, call whomever you like, it won't do you any good!

My sword is out, I'll use it to cut off your pretty
little head and kill you if you don't give up.
Stop if you want to live!

VASANTASENĀ Sir, I'm only a woman!

VIṬA That's why you're still alive!

SAMSTHĀNAKA Yes, that's why we didn't kill you.

VASANTASENĀ *[to herself]* He frightens me even when he tries to calm me! There seems no way.
*[aloud]* Sir, is it my jewels you want?

VIṬA Not at all! Lady Vasantasenā, the vine in the garden should keep its flowers. We don't want your jewels!

VASANTASENĀ Then what do you want?

SAMSTHĀNAKA I'm a real nobleman and can love like a god! I want you to love me.

VASANTASENĀ *[angrily]* Heaven forbid! You want me to do something that's quite beneath me.

VIṬA Vasantasenā, what you say isn't in keeping with your profession.

The courtesan's house is the haven of youth,
she's a vine that grows by the side of the road,
Your body is something that's bought and sold
You should welcome every man alike.
Noble and base, wise and fool,

All bathe in the same pool.
The peacock and the ugly crow
both bend the same branch low.
The ship that brings great men to port
also carries the common sort.
You are the pool, the branch, the ship;
if you pick and choose, you lose your grip.

VASANTASENĀ You can only rouse love by kindness, you can't get it by force.

SAṂSTHĀNAKA Viṭa, Viṭa, the fact is that ever since this slut saw Cārudatta in the garden of the Temple of Love, she's been devoted to the penniless beggar, and she won't have anything to do with me. That's his house over there on the left! We must see that she doesn't give us the slip.

VIṬA [*aside*] The fool always blurts out what he ought to keep to himself! So Vasantasenā's in love with Cārudatta, is she? It's true then that one pearl matches another. Oh well, who minds that? I've had enough of this idiot. [*aloud*] Did you say Cārudatta's house was on the left?

SAṂSTHĀNAKA That's right. Over there on the left!

VASANTASENĀ [*to herself*] How surprising! Cārudatta's house is here on the left. The wretch who insulted me has helped me after all, because now I can see the man I love.

VIṬA Now it's pitch dark!

Suddenly I am blind with the fall of darkness;
the darkness closes my open eyes. It seems
as though the dark clings to my body, the sky
is raining soot, the eyesight is quite useless
just like the service of this base-born rogue.

SAṂSTHĀNAKA I *must* catch her.

VIṬA Why, have you something to go by, you silly bastard!

SAṂSTHĀNAKA Go by! What's that?

VIṬA By the tinkling of her jewelry and the perfume of her garland.

SAṂSTHĀNAKA Of course! I can hear the perfume of her garland, but my nose is so full of darkness I can't see the tinkle of her jewelry at all!

VIṬA
Vasantasenā!
Maybe the darkness of the night conceals you
like lightning hidden in the womb of cloud,
but the perfume of your garland will betray you,
my Lady, and the tinkling of your anklets.

VASANTASENĀ [*aside*] Thanks for the warning! [*She removes her anklets and garlands and gropes her way.*] This is the way, I think I can feel it with my hands. This must be his side door. Oh, but it's locked.

CĀRUDATTA [*returns to the room*] My friend, I've finished my prayers. Now will you go and make an offering to the Mothers for me?

MAITREYA No, I won't!

CĀRUDATTA
How hard it is when a man grows poor—his kinsmen
won't heed his word; acquaintances will turn
their backs upon him, and his friends are few.
Nobody wants to meet him, no one talks to him
even out of politeness; at a rich man's party
they look at him with scorn; and in the highroad,
conscious of his shabby clothes, he keeps his distance
from the respectable. In my opinion
poverty is one of the most deadly sins.
Poverty! I pity you that cling to me.
I've nothing to give you while I am alive,
and when I'm dead what other man will have you?

MAITREYA [*embarrassed*] All right I'll go. But if I've got to go let me take Radanikā with me.

CĀRUDATTA [*calls*] Radanikā. I want you to go with Maitreya.

RADANIKĀ Yes, master, I'll go.

MAITREYA Radanikā, you hold the offerings and the light, while I open the side door [*does so*].

VASANTASENĀ Why, the door is opening as though to welcome me! I'll go in right away! Oh dear, there's a light! [*She blows it out* and goes in.*]

CĀRUDATTA What's happened, Maitreya?

MAITREYA Only a gust of wind blew the light out as I opened the door. Radanikā, you go on, while I go back and light the lamp.

[*Radanikā goes out into the street where the three are still groping for Vasantasenā.*]

SAṂSTHĀNAKA I've got her! I've got her!!

VIṬA You've got me, you idiot!

SAṂSTHĀNAKA Out of the way then, keep on one side! Now, I've got her!

SLAVE Master, it's me.

SAṂSTHĀNAKA Both of you keep out of the way. [*He seizes Radanikā by the hair.*] Now I've really got her, I've got Vasantasenā!

RADANIKĀ [*frightened*] Gentlemen! What are you doing to me?

VIṬA That's not her voice, you silly bastard!

SAṂSTHĀNAKA Cats mew differently when they want cream! It's that daughter of a slave-girl all right, but her voice has changed.

VIṬA What, changed her voice? That's strange! But after all it's not really surprising.

She's been on the stage, and she knows all the tricks.
She could well change her voice to get out of a fix.

* Original: "puts it out with the end of her *sari.*"

[*Maitreya comes out with a lighted lamp.*]

MAITREYA Strange. In the gentle evening breeze the flame of the lamp is trembling like the heart of a goat being led to the sacrifice.

SAṂSTHĀNAKA Viṭa, Viṭa! A man—it's a man!

MAITREYA It's neither right nor proper that strangers should trespass on Cārudatta's property, even if he is poor.

RADANIKĀ Master Maitreya! See how he laid his hands on me!!

MAITREYA [*angrily raising his staff*] Stop that! Even a dog is fiercest in his own kennel—and I'm a Brahman. My stick is as twisted as my fate, but if you don't stop I'll use it to crack open your head, which anyway is as hollow as a dry bamboo!

VIṬA Great Brahman, please forgive us.

MAITREYA You Saṃsthānaka, though you're the king's brother-in-law, you're a bad lot and what you've done isn't right and proper. Lord Cārudatta may have fallen on evil days, but his goodness is a credit to the city of Ujjain. So you must trespass on his property and misuse his servant girl!

VIṬA Sir, we beg your pardon. It didn't happen out of arrogance on our part—we just thought she was someone else.

> You see we were chasing a lady of doubtful virtue,
> driven by lust; and by mistake we caught
> this girl, and so we have abused her cruelly.

Please accept this proof of our regret for what we've done!

[*Throws away his sword and falls at Maitreya's feet.*]

MAITREYA Please get up. I see you're an honorable man. I spoke harshly because I didn't know the sort of man you were. Now that I do know, it's my turn to beg your pardon.

VIṬA No, you're the one who has most to forgive; so I'll stand up only on one condition.

MAITREYA What's that?

VIṬA That you won't tell Cārudatta what's happened.

MAITREYA All right! I won't tell him!

VIṬA I am a captive, good Brahman, at the feet of your kindness. We are men of the sword subdued by the sword of your virtue!

SAṂSTHĀNAKA [*annoyed*] Viṭa, why did you throw yourself at the feet of that clown and clasp your hands as if you were praying to him?

VIṬA I'm afraid.

SAṂSTHĀNAKA What's there to be afraid of?

VIṬA The virtue of Cārudatta.

SAṂSTHĀNAKA Whatever virtue is there in a man who hasn't a crumb in his house.

VIṬA You shouldn't say such things.

He has grown lean in helping such as us.
When he was rich, no one was turned away.
He's like a pool of water in the summer
that's now drained dry to slake the thirst of men.

SAṂSTHĀNAKA Who is he anyway, that son of a slave-girl?

VIṬA

A tree of bounty to the poor, he bent
under the weight of his own fruit, a friend
of all good men, a bright mirror of learning,
criterion of good conduct, the high-watermark of virtue,
beneficent, not haughty, a treasure of human virtues.
He truly *lives*—others merely breathe.

Let's go now!

SAṂSTHĀNAKA Without catching Vasantasenā? I won't budge without her!

VIṬA Didn't you ever hear the saying:

A chain controls an elephant,
a bridle holds a horse,

but love restrains a woman—
you can't keep *her* by force.

SAṂSTHĀNAKA All right—go if you like! But I stay here!

VIṬA Very well! I'm off! [*Exit.*]

SAṂSTHĀNAKA Good riddance! And as for you, you bald-headed lump of holiness, you go and tell your poverty-stricken Cārudatta that the courtesan Vasantasenā, dressed up in all her jewels like the leading lady on the first night of a new play, has got into his house, just as we were forcibly persuading her to come along with us. I know she's been in love with him ever since she first set eyes on him in the garden of the Temple of Love. If he'll hand her over to me, without making a fuss and without my having to take the matter to court, he may be sure of my friendship. If he won't I'm his enemy for life . . . You'll say it clearly, you'll say it firmly, and moreover you'll say it so distinctly that I can hear you when I'm sitting by the dovecote on the terrace of my palace. If you don't I'll crack your head like a nut in the jamb of a door!

MAITREYA All right, I'll tell him!

SAṂSTHĀNAKA [*to the slave*] Has Viṭa really gone?

SLAVE Yes, sir!

SAṂSTHĀNAKA Then let's get out of here right away! [*They start to go.*]

SLAVE Will you take your sword, master?

SAṂSTHĀNAKA You carry it.

SLAVE Your sword, master! Take it!

SAṂSTHĀNAKA [*takes the sword by the wrong end*]

I now take up my sword, red as a radish,
asleep within its sheath upon my shoulder,
and, like a jackal chased by yapping curs
and bitches, I seek shelter in my lair! [*Exeunt.*]

MAITREYA Radanikā, you mustn't let Master Cārudatta know how they insulted you. He has enough trouble already and this would make him twice as miserable.

RADANIKĀ I know how to hold my tongue, Master Maitreya!

MAITREYA Good!

CĀRUDATTA *[Inside the house, to Vasantasenā, not looking at her]* Radanikā, Rohasena is outside. He loves playing in the wind, but the evening's turning cold. Go and bring him in, and wrap him in this cloak *[holds it out]*.

VASANTASENĀ *[to herself]* He thinks I'm the servant. *[She takes the cloak, and smells it.]* It's scented with jasmine! That shows he hasn't quite forgotten how to live! *[She puts on the cloak.]*

*[Enter Maitreya and Radanikā. Cārudatta still does not look up, and does not notice them.]*

CĀRUDATTA Go on, Radanikā, go and fetch Rohasena and bring him into the house.

VASANTASENĀ *[aside]* Oh, I wish I could get into his heart as well as his house.

CĀRUDATTA What's the matter, Radanikā? Why don't you answer me? *[to himself]*

When a man falls, through adverse destiny,
on evil days, his friends all turn to foes,
and even his loyal servants lose their manners.

MAITREYA Here's Radanikā, old friend.

CĀRUDATTA Radanikā! Then who's that other woman? *[He turns and sees Vasantasenā.]*

In my distraction I defiled her with the touch of my
garment and she wears it, standing half in shadow,
she's like the new moon of autumn, veiled by a cloud.

But I ought not even to look at another man's wife.

MAITREYA No need for scruples on that score! She's Vasantasenā the courtesan and she's been in love with you ever since the day she first saw you in the garden of the Temple of Love.

CĀRUDATTA *[aside]* Vasantasenā!

MAITREYA And what's more I've got a message about her from the king's brother-in-law.

CĀRUDATTA Oh! What is it?

MAITREYA He saw Vasantasenā had slipped into the house while he was after her. If you send her to him without trouble he'll be your friend, but if not he's your enemy for life!

CĀRUDATTA *[aloud]* Crazy idiot!
*[to himself]* I could worship this woman as a goddess!

"Come home with me," he urged. She wouldn't go,
for all his wealth and power. She knows her men! With
me she is modestly silent, though much is spoken.

CĀRUDATTA *[aloud]* Lady Vasantasenā, I'm sorry I treated you with disrespect, when I mistook you for the servant. I bow my head and ask your pardon!

VASANTASENĀ I'm the culprit coming into your house without permission. So I bow my head and ask *your* pardon.

MAITREYA Look at the two of them, bowing their heads in unison like two rice-fields in the wind. Now I'll bow my head, like a knock-kneed camel, and ask both your pardons.

CĀRUDATTA Let's dispense with formality and be friends.

VASANTASENĀ *[to herself]* What a pleasant and delightful suggestion. But I ought not to stay the night in a house where I've not been invited. I know what I'll say.
*[aloud]* Sir, if you want to do me a favor, please let me leave these jewels I'm wearing here. I think those crooks only followed me because of my jewels.

CĀRUDATTA This house is hardly worthy of such a trust.

VASANTASENĀ You're wrong, sir! Trust is placed in men, not in houses.

CĀRUDATTA Maitreya, please take the jewels!

VASANTASENĀ I'm really grateful to you! [*She hands over her jewels.*]

MAITREYA [*taking them*] Thank you, madam.

CĀRUDATTA You silly fool! She's just leaving them with us for safe keeping!

MAITREYA [*aside, disappointed*] If that's the case, let the thieves come and get them for all I care!

CĀRUDATTA Very soon—

MAITREYA [*aside*] What we have ought to be ours.

CĀRUDATTA . . . I'll hand them back.

[*Maitreya hands the jewels to Cārudatta, who puts them in a small gold box.*]

VASANTASENĀ Sir, I'd be very glad if this gentleman would see me home.

CĀRUDATTA Maitreya, see this lady home.

MAITREYA You should go with her—you'd look like a royal swan with his mate. The mob would yap around me like dogs round a bit of meat.

CĀRUDATTA All right, I'll go too. Have the lanterns lighted. We don't want trouble on the highway.

MAITREYA Vardhamānaka!

[*Vardhamānaka enters.*]

MAITREYA Light the lanterns.

VARDHAMĀNAKA Without oil, sir?

MAITREYA Would you believe it? Our lamps are just like prostitutes! They'll have no truck with penniless lovers. They won't burn without oil.

CĀRUDATTA It's all right, Maitreya, we shan't need them.

The moon is rising, pale as the cheek of a girl
in love, with its train of stars to light our road.
Its white rays fall on the darkness all around,
like a stream of milk upon a muddy pool.

[*They walk through the streets.*]

CĀRUDATTA Lady Vasantasenā, here's your home! Won't you go in?

[*She looks at him longingly, and goes in.*]

CĀRUDATTA Now she's gone, my friend. Let's go home.

The King's highway is empty, but for the tramp
of watchmen on their rounds; this is no time
for longing, many dangers lurk at night.

[*as they walk*] Maitreya, tonight you must guard this box of jewels. Vardhamānaka will take charge of it tomorrow.

MAITREYA All right, sir, I will.

# Act II

*Next day. Vasantasenā's house and the street outside. Vasantasenā enters followed by Madanikā.*

MADANIKĀ Please don't be offended. You know it's affection and not impertinence that makes me ask, but whatever is the matter?

VASANTASENĀ What do you think is the matter Madanikā?

MADANIKĀ You're so absentminded I'd say you'd lost your heart.

VASANTASENĀ And so I have! You're a good judge of other people's feelings, Madanikā.

MADANIKĀ I'm glad! Incidentally, the name of the god concerned with your case is—love, and young people delight in his festivals! But tell me, is it the king or one of his courtiers you're thinking of?

VASANTASENĀ My girl, I'm thinking now in terms of love, not business!

MADANIKĀ Well then, perhaps you're in love with a brilliant scholarly young Brahman!

VASANTASENĀ I respect learned Brahmans, but I don't fall in love with them!

MADANIKĀ So perhaps you're in love with a young merchant who's traveled from city to city and made a pile of money.

VASANTASENĀ My girl, if I fell in love with a merchant he'd soon leave me, no matter how much I loved him, to go on his travels, and that would make me very, very miserable!

MADANIKĀ Well, if he's not the king, not a courtier, not a Brahman, and not a merchant, who can it be you're in love with?

VASANTASENĀ You were with me, weren't you, when I went to the Temple of Love a few days ago?

MADANIKĀ Yes ma'am, of course I was.

VASANTASENĀ And yet you don't seem to know anything!

MADANIKĀ [*suddenly realizing*] Now I know! The same man who so kindly sheltered you in his home.

VASANTASENĀ Do you know his name?

MADANIKĀ Yes, he lives in the Square of the Merchants.

VASANTASENĀ But his name?

MADANIKĀ His name's Cārudatta. A pleasant-sounding name, isn't it?

VASANTASENĀ [*happily*] Well done, Madanikā! You know a lot.

MADANIKĀ [*aside*] I certainly do.
[*aloud*] But they say he's poor!

VASANTASENĀ Perhaps that's why I love him—though you don't often hear of a courtesan who falls in love with a man with no money!

MADANIKĀ But bees don't buzz round a mango tree when there aren't any flowers.

VASANTASENĀ That's because they're only interested in getting honey!

MADANIKĀ If you're so much in love with him, why don't you go and see him straightaway?

VASANTASENĀ Not just yet. There are difficulties in the way, but I've a plan.

MADANIKĀ Ah! I see now why you left your jewels with him!

VASANTASENĀ You're right again, my girl!

VOICES OFF Stop that man! He's lost ten gold pieces at dice and won't pay up. Stop him! Stop him!

*[Saṃvāhaka*—enters, frightened.]*

SAṂVĀHAKA Oh, how hard is the life of a gambler!
While he reckoned up the score, I slipped quietly outside,
Now they're hot on my heels, and I've nowhere to hide!

*[He looks about him and sees a half-ruined roadside shrine, from which the image has been removed.]*

I know what I'll do. I'll walk backward into the shrine, and make a god of myself!

*[He does so, sitting cross-legged on the empty dais in the shrine.]*

*[Enter Māthura, the keeper of the gambling house, and a Gambler.]*

MĀTHURA Stop him! Stop him! He owes me ten gold pieces in gambling debts. Stop! Stop!! I can see you over there!

GAMBLER You may hide in the deepest hell, or in Indra's heaven, but Śiva himself can't save you from the master of the gambling den, when you haven't paid your debts.

MĀTHURA
You swindler of an honest gaming-house,
You're scared! Your body's shuddering with fright!
You stumble at every step! I know you're near,
you blackener of the honor of your family!

GAMBLER *[sees a footprint]* Look, this is the way he came. There's his footprint.

MĀTHURA *[looks at the ground thoughtfully]* Why! The footprints go back to that shrine over there! There wasn't an image in it when I last came this way! I fancy he walked into it backward.

---

* This, like *viṭa,* is not strictly a proper name. It means "masseur."

GAMBLER Let's go over and have a look.

*[They go over to the shrine, and show by their gestures that they have detected the fugitive.]*

GAMBLER Is this a wooden image?

MĀTHURA I should say it's stone. [*They poke Saṃvāhaka.*] Who cares anyway! Come on, let's have a game!

*[They sit on the ground and play dice at the feet of the idol.]*

SAṂVĀHAKA [*trying hard to resist the temptation to join in*] [*aside*] The rattle of the dice tears the heart out of the man who can't afford a stake, like the roll of the drum to a king who's lost his throne. I swear I'll never play again, for if I did I might as well throw myself from the peak of the highest mountain. But oh how sweet that sound to my heart, like the call of the cuckoo!

GAMBLER Now it's my turn!

MĀTHURA No, it's mine!

SAṂVĀHAKA [*jumps down from the dais*] No, it's not, it's mine!

GAMBLER [*seizing Saṃvāhaka*] Now we've got him!

MĀTHURA So, you cheat, where are those ten gold pieces?

SAṂVĀHAKA I'll be sure and give them to you today.

MĀTHURA I want them this minute!

SAṂVĀHAKA I *will* pay you, if only you'll be kind to me and give me time!

MĀTHURA No! You'll pay up now. [*They force him to the ground and beat him.*]

SAṂVĀHAKA [*gets to his feet, sadly*] I know gambling debts are debts of honor, but I just can't pay!
[*to the Gambler, without Māthura hearing*] I'll give you half if you'll let me off the rest.

GAMBLER All right then!

SAṂVĀHAKA *[to Māthura quietly, without the Gambler hearing]* I'll give you half, if you'll let me off the rest!

MĀTHURA I suppose half's better than nothing. I agree!

SAṂVĀHAKA *[aloud]* Good! Now, sir, you have let me off paying half, haven't you?

MĀTHURA Yes!

SAṂVĀHAKA *[to the Gambler]* And you've let me off half?

GAMBLER I have!

SAṂVĀHAKA That's just fine. Now I'll be off! *[Starts to leave.]*

MĀTHURA Hey, where are you going? Pay up your debts first.

SAṂVĀHAKA What's wrong? Look, you let me off five, and *you* let me off five so I don't owe you anything. That's fair enough!

MĀTHURA *[seizing him again]* You cheat! I'll have you know that my name's Māthura, and you can't get away with your tricks when Māthura's about. So, you swindler, you're going to pay me every one of those gold pieces right now.

SAṂVĀHAKA Where am I to get them?

MĀTHURA Sell your father if need be, but pay up!

SAṂVĀHAKA I haven't got a father.

MĀTHURA Well then, sell your mother!

SAṂVĀHAKA I haven't any mother, either.

MĀTHURA All right then, you'll just have to sell yourself!

SAṂVĀHAKA Give me time, won't you? Very well, take me to the main street.

MĀTHURA Come on then!

*[They walk across the stage.]*

SAṂVĀHAKA [*loudly*] Who will buy me from this man for ten gold pieces? You, sir. What can I do to make myself useful? I can do all sorts of housework! No good! I'll try another. [*shouting*] Who will buy me for ten gold pieces! Oh, it's no good! No one wants me! Oh how hard it's been for me since Cārudatta lost his money. Sure he'd help me pay if he could!

MĀTHURA So you won't pay up, then?

[*He pulls him to the ground and starts beating him again.*]

SAṂVĀHAKA Help! Help!

[*Enter Darduraka.*]

DARDURAKA What's going on here? Why, it's that swindler Māthura. He's beaten the poor fellow black and blue. Hey, Māthura, what's this all about?

MĀTHURA [*stops beating Saṃvāhaka*] It's Darduraka. He's gambled ten gold pieces a thousand times and lost the lot. [*to Darduraka*] He owes me ten gold pieces.

DARDURAKA Well I suggest you lend him another ten pieces, and let him try his luck with them. If he wins he'll pay you back what he owes.

MĀTHURA And if he doesn't?

DARDURAKA Why, he won't pay, of course!

MĀTHURA Clever, aren't you? Why don't *you* lend him ten pieces, while you're about it, you useless loafer? Saṃvāhaka, I want my ten gold pieces!

SAṂVĀHAKA I'll give them to you today. I promise.

[*Māthura again starts beating Saṃvāhaka.*]

DARDURAKA You fool! You won't beat him like that while I'm looking on!

*[Māthura punches Saṃvāhaka hard on the nose, and he falls to the ground, bleeding and unconscious. Darduraka comes up and tries to hold Māthura off. Māthura strikes him and he strikes back.]*

MĀTHURA You bloody son of a whore! You'll get what's coming to you for this.

DARDURAKA You idiot—you've struck an inoffensive passerby. Tomorrow in the court you'll see what happens if you try that one again!

MĀTHURA Yes, I'll see. This is how I'll see.

*[He thrusts his face at Darduraka and glares at him, his eyes wide open. Darduraka quickly picks up a handful of dust and throws it in Māthura's face, signaling to Saṃvāhaka, who has regained consciousness, to escape. Māthura, his hands to his eyes, slips and falls.]*

DARDURAKA *[aside]* He's got the biggest gambling place in town and now I've made him my enemy! I'd best get out of here! My friend Śarvilaka tells me that a cowherd's son named Āryaka is raising a revolt in the provinces and lots of men like us are joining the rebels. I think I'd better join them too! *[Exit.]*

SAṂVĀHAKA *[nervously]* There's a house with the door open. I'd better go in. *[He sees Vasantasenā.]* Lady, help me please!

VASANTASENĀ You're safe with me. *[to Madanikā]* Madanikā, shut the door! *[She does so.]*
*[to Saṃvāhaka]* What's given you such a fright?

SAṂVĀHAKA A man I owe some money to, lady!

VASANTASENĀ If that's all there is to it, you can open the door again, Madanikā!

SAṂVĀHAKA *[aside]* Why, she isn't in the least afraid of creditors!

The man whose burden is not greater than
his back can carry, will not trip or fall,
and through rough places he passes safe and sound.

[*Outside Māthura rubs his eyes.*]

MĀTHURA [*thinking he is speaking to Saṃvāhaka*] Come on now, pay up!

GAMBLER Sir, while we were fighting with Darduraka the fellow gave us the slip!

MĀTHURA I smashed his nose with my fist! Come on, we can track him down by the trail of blood!

GAMBLER Look! He's gone into Vasantasenā's house!

MĀTHURA Then that's the end of my ten gold pieces.

GAMBLER Let's go and lay a complaint in court.

MĀTHURA Then he'll come out and go off. No, we'll only get him if we lie in wait till he shows up.

[*Vasantasenā gives a sign to Madanikā.*]

MADANIKĀ Sir, we'd like you to tell us where you're from, who you are, what's your job, and the real reason you were so frightened.

SAṂVĀHAKA All right, I'll tell you! I was born in Patna, I'm the son of a respectable householder, and I'm a masseur by trade!

VASANTASENĀ It's a pleasant art you have learned!

SAṂVĀHAKA When I was young, travelers would come to our house and tell stories about other lands, and so I wanted to see them myself! So in the end I came to Ujjain and got a job as private masseur to a gentleman in these parts. He was so good natured and well spoken, and he didn't boast of his own generosity or remember wrongs done to him in the past. He always treated others as he would himself, and he never turned down anyone who asked his help!

MADANIKĀ Who can this paragon of virtue be? He seems to have stolen the good qualities of the man my mistress loves.

VASANTASENĀ How right you are, my girl, how right you are! That's just what I was thinking.

MADANIKĀ And then?

SAṂVĀHAKA Then, through his unfortunate generosity . . .

VASANTASENĀ He lost all his money, eh?

SAṂVĀHAKA How did you anticipate what I was going to say, lady?

VASANTASENĀ It was obvious! You don't often find goodness and money together.

MADANIKĀ Sir, what's his name?

SAṂVĀHAKA Lady, who doesn't know his name? He lives in the Square of the Merchants, and his name is Master Cārudatta!

VASANTASENĀ *[rising from her seat with pleasure]* Sir, this house is yours! Madanikā, give him a seat and fan him! Can't you see how tired he is?

SAṂVĀHAKA *[aside]* Just because I mentioned Cārudatta's name they treat me like a lord. Good for you, Master Cārudatta! You're the only man on earth who really lives—the others merely breathe.
*[to Vasantasenā]* Please don't get up, lady. You sit down. I'm all right standing up.

VASANTASENĀ *[sitting down]* Now, tell me about this creditor of yours.

SAṂVĀHAKA Well, I was in Cārudatta's service till he was left with nothing but his virtue! Then I took to living by my wits, and became a professional gambler. Now my luck's against me, and I've lost ten gold pieces.

MĀTHURA *[shouts, outside]* I've been ruined! I've been robbed!

SAṂVĀHAKA That's the keeper of the gaming house and the gambler who were after me. Won't you help me!

VASANTASENĀ Madanikā, go and give this bracelet to those two men outside, and tell them that this gentleman here sent it!
*[She takes off her bracelet and gives it to Madanikā.]*

MADANIKĀ *[taking it]* Very well. *[She goes out.]*
*[to Māthura]* Good day, gentlemen!

MĀTHURA And good day to you.

MADANIKĀ Sirs, which of you keeps a gambling house?

MĀTHURA
To whom, slim girl whose lips are scarred by teeth
of other lovers, do you speak such charming and
gentle words, with fluttering sidelong glances?

MADANIKĀ Why can't he give me a straight answer? I think a man owes one of you some money.

MĀTHURA That's right. There's a man who owes me ten gold pieces. Do you know anything about him?

MADANIKĀ I do indeed. My mistress sends you this bracelet—no, no! I mean he sends it himself!

MĀTHURA [*excitedly snatching the bracelet*] Good! Now tell the gentleman that we're quits, and I'll be glad to see him again in my place whenever he feels like enjoying a little game! [*Exit with the Gambler. Madanikā returns.*]

MADANIKĀ They're quite satisfied now and they've both gone off!

VASANTASENĀ [*to Saṃvāhaka*] Now you must go and put your family's minds at rest!

SAṂVĀHAKA Lady, you've been so good to me. Can I pay you back by showing some of my skill with my hands?

VASANTASENĀ Sir, you ought to use your skill only for the man you worked for in the past, who had you trained in the art of massage.

SAṂVĀHAKA [*aside*] How gracefully she's let me off my debt to her. There's really no other way I can pay her back. [*aloud*] Lady, I'm fed up with the life of a gambler. I've made up my mind to become a Buddhist monk! Please remember always when the wretched masseur-turned-gambler took to the life of religion.

VASANTASENĀ Sir—I advise you not to make a rash decision.

SAṂVĀHAKA No, my mind's quite made up!

As a gambler, I was scorned by everyone.
Now, shaven-headed, I shall walk the highway
with dignity, and win the world's respect!

# Act III

*The same night. Cārudatta's house and the street outside. Enter Vardhamānaka, preparing two beds.*

VARDHAMĀNAKA It's past midnight and Cārudatta hasn't come back from the concert. While I'm waiting I'll go and have a nap in the hall [*does so*].

[*Cārudatta and Maitreya appear outside the house.*]

CĀRUDATTA Oh, how well Rebhila sang tonight! And surely the lute is a pearl among the instruments.

It is a friend who feels for man's distress,
the best of pastimes when a man waits long
to meet his darling; it comforts parted lovers,
and makes their passion and their joy more strong.

MAITREYA Come on! Let's go home!

CĀRUDATTA But really, Rebhila sang *so* beautifully. Weren't you delighted with him?

MAITREYA Look, even the dogs are fast asleep in the doors of the shops! And the moon is leaving its palace in the sky, and giving the world over to darkness! Well, here we are. [*calling*] Vardhamānaka, Vardhamānaka, open the door!

VARDHAMĀNAKA [*opens the door*] Good evening, sirs. I've made your beds. Will you sit down? [*They do so.*]

MAITREYA Vardhamānaka, call Radanikā and tell her to come and wash our feet.

CĀRUDATTA No. She's asleep; don't wake her up!

VARDHAMĀNAKA I'll fetch the water, sir! But first I must give Master Maitreya this jewel box, which you said I was to guard by day and he by night! [*Does so; exits.*]

MAITREYA What! It's still here then! Isn't there one thief in the whole city of Ujjain who'll steal this bastard of a box which robs me of my sleep? I think I'll put it in the inner room.

CĀRUDATTA No, don't put it there. We are holding it in trust for Vasantasenā, so you must take full charge of it yourself till it's given back to her.

MAITREYA [*showing signs of drowsiness*] Are you feeling sleepy?

CĀRUDATTA

Sleep seems to flow down, pouring over my forehead
and hanging in drops upon my heavy eyelids.
It comes like the insidious and unseen
coming of old age, to sap a man's vitality.

MAITREYA Let's sleep then! [*They do so.*]

[*Enter the burglar Śarvilaka, stealthily creeping on the ground.*]

ŚARVILAKA

I made a hole in the wall that I can squeeze
through, in the course of business, thanks to my
strength and training. It scrapes my haunches as I
wriggle through it, like a snake that leaves behind
its outgrown skin.

[*looks up*]

Good—the moon is setting!
The stars are covered by darkness, dense and heavy.
A night like this is a mother to such as I—
brave resolute men, who pillage other men's houses,
always on the lookout for the city watch!

Well, here I am in the garden! Now I must get into the house. Where shall I make a hole? [*feels along the wall*] Here's a place that's a bit exposed to full sunlight and heavy rain, where the wall's a bit weak. And here's a rat hole. Just what I wanted. A sign that the god of thieves loves his favorite son! Now what sort of hole shall I make? As I remember it, Kanakaśakti's *Manual of Burglary* lists four ways of making a hole in a wall: pulling out baked bricks, cutting through unbaked bricks, softening mud walls by wetting them, and sawing through wooden ones. These are baked bricks, so I must loosen them and pull them out! . . . I'll make a good job of it, and show such skill as will tomorrow amaze citizens.
[*Before he starts work he prays, with joined palms.*]
Reverence to Kārtikeya, the god of thieves; reverence to the teachers of kleptology in ancient days—Kanakaśakti, Brahmaṇyadeva Devavrata and Bhāskaranandī; and reverence to my venerable teacher Yogācārya, whose chief pupil I am.
[*normal voice*]

It was he who gave me a magic salve
because he was so pleased with my progress.
When I anoint myself no guard can see me,
no weapons, however sharp, can even scratch me.

[*He starts to work.*] Blast it! I've forgotten my tapemeasure. Never mind—I'll use my sacred cord. Since I was initiated as a Brahman in my boyhood I've worn it constantly, as a good Brahman should. Of course I'm not supposed ever to take it off, but on the quiet it's often come in useful! Indeed it's particularly helpful to men of my profession:

With it I can measure a wall to make an opening;
it serves to lasso things kept out of reach;
it can be helpful in picking difficult locks;
and acts as a tourniquet in cases of snakebite!

Well, now to the job! [*He works at the wall—pausing.*] Just one brick more and it's done! [*He looks through the hole.*]

It's done at last! Now I'm going in. [*Again joins his palms in prayer.*] Reverence to Kārtikeya, god of thieves. [*Crawls through and looks round.*] Hm—two men asleep! I'll open the door, just in case I have to run for it! [*does so*] Now I'd better see if they're really asleep or just pretending. [*He pulls ugly faces at them.*] No, they are really asleep! [*He looks around.*] A drum, a lute, a flute, some books. This must be the house of a music teacher! I decided on this job because from outside it looked like a rich man's place, but they're really quite poor, or perhaps they've buried their valuables for fear of the government or of burglars.

MAITREYA [*talking in his sleep*] I say old man, there's a hole in the wall. Look, there's a thief. You take this golden box!

ŚARVILAKA I wonder whether he's seen me and is making fun of me, because they're so poor. If that's how it is I'll kill him! But perhaps he's dreaming. [*Looks at Maitreya closely.*] But what's this? It really is a golden box full of lady's ornaments, wrapped in a bit of old bathrobe! That's something worth having at least! But I don't know! After all they're not better off than I am, and it wouldn't be fair to make things harder for them. I think I'll go!

MAITREYA [*still talking in his sleep*] Oh friend, if you don't take this golden box you'll be accursed, like the man who refuses the wish of a Brahman or tries to harm a sacred cow!

ŚARVILAKA When cows and Brahmans come into it I've no choice in the matter! I'll put out the light [*does so*]. Now it's dark. But what about the dark I've brought on myself and my Brahman family? Here am I, the Brahman Śarvilaka, the son of a Brahman who knew the four Vedas by heart, committing crimes for the sake of that little whore Madanikā! Anyway, there's no going back now. I may as well do what he wants me to do! [*Reaches for the casket and touches Maitreya.*]

MAITREYA I say old friend, your fingers are cold.

ŚARVILAKA [*startled*] Oh! That was careless of me! I'll warm my hand in my armpit first. [*Does so, and takes the casket.*]

MAITREYA [*still half asleep*] Have you got it?

ŚARVILAKA When a Brahman asks you to do something, you have to do it! Yes, got it!

MAITREYA Now I can sleep really soundly, like a shopkeeper who's sold all his stock.

ŚARVILAKA Master, may you sleep a hundred years. It's a shame that I have to ruin a respectable Brahman's house and my own soul into the bargain to get Madanikā; but needs must! Now I'm off to Vasantasenā's house to buy Madanikā's freedom . . . What's that sound! I hope it's not the watchman. I'll stand stock still and wait [*hides by wall*]. What do I care for watchmen?

I can climb like a cat, run like a deer, swoop down like a hawk,
I'm as brave as a mastiff, I can twist like a snake,
I've all sorts of disguises, I know every language,
I can see in the dark, I'm as strong as a horse,
I can swim like a fish, I'm as firm as a mountain.

[*The maid Radanikā enters.*]

RADANIKĀ What was that? I thought Vardhamānaka was asleep in the outer room. I'll call Master Maitreya.

ŚARVILAKA [*prepares to kill Radanikā, and stops short*] Why, it's only a girl! I'll be off! [*Exit*].

RADANIKĀ [*alarmed*] Help! Help! I'd better wake up Maitreya. [*Goes up to him and shouts.*] Wake up, Master Maitreya! I've just seen a burglar getting through in the wall!

MAITREYA [*waking sleepily*] What's that? What's that? Did I hear you say a hole had got through a burglar in the wall?

RADANIKĀ Oh! It's no laughing matter! Can't you see it?

MAITREYA Yes! Why, it looks like another door! Cārudatta, wake up! A burglar's just got through a hole in the wall!

CĀRUDATTA [*drowsily*] What's that? This is no time for jokes!

MAITREYA It's no joke, Cārudatta! Just look!

CĀRUDATTA [*sees hole*] My word! He made a really good job of it, didn't he!

MAITREYA Only two kinds of burglar would have made a hole like that—either one who's just arrived here from another town or one who is being trained in the art. Everyone in Ujjain knows we've nothing here worth stealing!

CĀRUDATTA

This hole was made by a well-trained foreigner
who did not know we slept the long, sound sleep
of poor men; for he saw the grand facade
and made his hole, and went back disappointed.

The poor chap will have to tell his friends how he entered the home of a merchant's son and didn't find anything worth stealing there!

MAITREYA What, you'll even sympathize with him! Of course he thought this was a rich man's home and he'd get away with boxes of jewels and gold . . . Boxes of jewels? That reminds me! Wasn't it a good thing I gave you that casket of jewels in the night? If I hadn't that slave-girl's son would have got it!

CĀRUDATTA I wish you'd stop joking, Maitreya!

MAITREYA Now look here, old man, I may be a fool, but I know the right time and place for making jokes! Don't you remember how I told you how cold your fingers were?

CĀRUDATTA Did you say that to me? I can't remember. [*He searches around the room.*] I've got some good news for you—the box has gone!

MAITREYA [*startled*] Well, what's good about that?

CĀRUDATTA At least the burglar got something for his trouble!

MAITREYA But it was left with us for safekeeping and now we've lost it.

CĀRUDATTA [*registers great distress**] Yes, it wasn't mine!

MAITREYA Cheer up, old man! It's not your own property that's been stolen, so why get so upset!

CĀRUDATTA
But who will believe a poor man such as I?
The world always suspects the penniless
So far my fate has only harmed my riches,
and now even my good name will be dishonored!

RADANIKĀ I'd better go and tell the mistress. [*Exit.*]

MAITREYA If I were you I'd deny everything—say you've never seen the box.

CĀRUDATTA Do you want me to tell an outright lie?
I'd rather beg, to pay back what was trusted to me,
than tell a lie and lose my self-respect.

[*They all go out. Radanikā returns with Dhūtā, Cārudatta's wife.*]

WIFE [*alarmed*] Is he alright? And is Maitreya safe?

RADANIKĀ Oh yes, ma'am, they're both safe and sound! But the courtesan's jewels have been stolen.

WIFE [*in great distress*] I'm glad he's not come to harm, but I'd rather his body had been hurt than his reputation! Now all Ujjain will be saying he took the jewels because he's so poor! Life is uncertain as a drop of water quivering on the tip of a lotus leaf! . . . Look, I brought this pearl necklace from my mother's house when I married my husband, but I hardly think he'd accept it if I offered it to him myself. My girl—call Master Maitreya will you?

RADANIKĀ Certainly, ma'am. [*calling*] Master Maitreya! The mistress wants you.

---

* In original, "faints."

MAITREYA [*comes up*] Here I am! [*to Wife*] Good morning, madam! I hope you're well!

WIFE Good morning, master! Now, I want you to look me straight in the face.

MAITREYA Right! [*Does so.*]

WIFE Now take this, sir! [*Gives him necklace.*]

MAITREYA What is it?

WIFE Today is the festival of jewels, when one should give jewels to the Brahmans, as far as one's wealth allows. That's why I want you to take these pearls.

MAITREYA [*seeing the point*] Thank you very much indeed, my lady. Now I'll go and tell my friend about my good luck!

WIFE Thank you, Master Maitreya—and I hope you'll tell him in a way that won't embarrass me. [*Exit.*]

MAITREYA What a wonderful woman she is!

[*Cārudatta comes in.*]

CĀRUDATTA What's keeping you, Maitreya? I hope you aren't letting our troubles lead you into doing anything dishonest.

MAITREYA I'm all right! Here you are [*giving the necklace*], it's all yours!

CĀRUDATTA [*looking at the necklace, surprised*] Where did this come from?

MAITREYA It's the reward of having a wife who's every bit as good as you are!

CĀRUDATTA So my wife has come to my help! But it's hard, all the same, for now I'm really and truly poor!

When a man's luck turns so bad that a woman's jewels
are all he has to help him out of trouble,
his poverty makes a woman of him, while a woman
through wealth becomes as powerful as a man.

Maitreya, take this necklace to Vasantasenā, and tell her that I hope she'll accept it in place of her jewels, because I forgot they were hers and lost them last night at gambling!

MAITREYA Surely you're not going to give this priceless necklace, the quintessence of the four oceans, in exchange for a few cheap trinkets which we never got any benefit from.

CĀRUDATTA Maitreya, you shouldn't say such things! Now, I solemnly command you—you will not come back here until you have given the necklace to Vasantasenā!
[*calling*] Vardhamānaka, get those bricks put back quickly before the neighbors start gossiping!
[*to Maitreya*] Now Maitreya, my old friend! Off you go, and mind you hold your head high when you speak to her—There's nothing to be shamefaced about!

MAITREYA But how can a poor person talk to a rich one without being shamefaced?

CĀRUDATTA *I'm* not poor, my friend!—

I've a wife who shares my troubles;
I've a good friend in need;
My honor is untarnished—
and this is wealth indeed!

So off you go now, while I bathe and say my morning prayers!

# Act IV

*Next morning. Vasantasenā's house. Vasantasenā is painting. Enter Madanikā.*

VASANTASENĀ Come here, Madanikā. Tell me, do you think this is a good likeness of Cārudatta?

MADANIKĀ [*looking*] Yes! I'd say it's a very good likeness.

VASANTASENĀ How do you know? You've hardly seen him.

MADANIKĀ I know it's a good likeness because you keep gazing at it so tenderly.

VASANTASENĀ But I don't think you mean what you say, my girl! You're just flattering, as courtesans are always taught to do!

MADANIKĀ Would you say then that serving a courtesan will always make one tell lies?

VASANTASENĀ I'm afraid so! You see, my girl, when you have to entertain so many men you inevitably get into the habit of flattering.

MADANIKĀ There's no need to ask why you can't take your eyes off that portrait.

VASANTASENĀ Yes! I can't help it! I'm afraid my friends in the profession will all laugh at me for falling in love.

MADANIKĀ Don't worry on that score. Women understand one another, whether they're in the profession or not!

[*Enter maid.*]

MAID Madam, there's a covered carriage waiting for you at the side door!

VASANTASENĀ Who sent it? Was it Master Cārudatta?

MAID Oh no, madam! The man who sent it has also sent a very valuable jewel that must be worth ten thousand gold pieces.

VASANTASENĀ Whoever could it be?

MAID It's the king's brother-in-law Saṃsthānaka, ma'am!

VASANTASENĀ [*angrily*] Get out, girl! And never let me hear you mention his name again!

MAID Oh, please don't be angry with me, ma'am. I only brought the message.

VASANTASENĀ It's the message that makes me so angry!

MAID Well, what am I to say, madam?

VASANTASENĀ Tell him that if I get any more messages of that kind, I'll kill myself!

MAID Just as you say, madam. [*Exit.*]

[*Enter Śarvilaka outside the house.*]

VASANTASENĀ [*to Madanikā*] Madanikā, please hang this picture over my bed, and bring me my fan.

MADANIKĀ Certainly. [*Exit.*]

ŚARVILAKA Well, here's Vasantasenā's house. I'll go in [*does so*]. Now where can I find Madanikā?

[*Madanikā comes in, carrying a fan.*]

ŚARVILAKA Why, here she is!

To me she's like the goddess of love herself.
Like sandal she cools my body, afire with passion.

MADANIKĀ Why, if it isn't Śarvilaka! Hello, Śarvilaka, what have you been up to lately?

ŚARVILAKA I'll tell you, darling. [*They look affectionately at one another.*]

VASANTASENĀ [*in the room, while Madanikā and Śarvilaka are in the courtyard*] Madanikā has been gone a long time. I wonder where she can be! [*looks out of the window*] Why, there she is, talking to a man! From the way they're looking at one another with such affection it's evidently the man she was talking about, who wants to buy her freedom. Let them enjoy themselves! One should never interfere with the course of true love! I won't call her!

[*Śarvilaka looks around him suspiciously.*]

MADANIKĀ [*alarmed*] Śarvilaka, why are you so nervous?

ŚARVILAKA I'll tell you a secret! Are we alone here?

MADANIKĀ Of course!

VASANTASENĀ If it's a lovers' secret I ought not to listen.

ŚARVILAKA Madanikā, would Vasantasenā set you free if I paid her?

VASANTASENĀ It seems it involves me, so I will listen.

MADANIKĀ Śarvilaka, the mistress says that if she had full control of the establishment, she'd set all her servants free. But she hasn't, so where can you get the money to buy me from her?

ŚARVILAKA Oppressed by poverty and fired by love,
last night for your sake I committed crime.

MADANIKĀ Śarvilaka, up till now you always seemed a respectable man to me. Now you confess to committing a serious crime and breaking all the rules of good behavior for my sake.

ŚARVILAKA You must know that I'm a trained professional thief. But I won't have it that I'm a bad lot.

I never rob a woman of her jewels
for she's a vine in flower, nor do I take
the money paid to priests for sacrifice.
I never kidnap children for a ransom.
Though I'm a thief, I still know right from wrong!

Now I want you to take these jewels to Vasantasenā and ask her to accept them in payment for your freedom.

MADANIKĀ [*very worried*] First let me see them!

ŚARVILAKA [*suspiciously hands them to her*] Here they are.

MADANIKĀ [*looking at them*] I think I've seen those jewels before somewhere. Tell me where you got them!

ŚARVILAKA What does it matter, Madanikā? Take them!

MADANIKĀ [*angrily*] If you don't trust me, then why do you want to have me set free to marry you?

ŚARVILAKA Well if you *must* know, I stole them from the house of a merchant Cārudatta!

[*Both Madanikā and Vasantasenā display great distress.**]

ŚARVILAKA [*alarmed*] Madanikā! What's the matter?

Your body is limp with fear, your eyes swim with distress.
Your freedom is in sight, and you tremble, but not with joy!

MADANIKĀ You're a criminal! Was anyone in the house killed or injured?

ŚARVILAKA Madanikā! I don't harm people who are scared or asleep! I did no bodily injury to anyone.

* Literally, "faint."

MADANIKĀ Are you quite sure?

ŚARVILAKA Of course I'm sure!

VASANTASENĀ [*with a sigh of relief*] I can breathe again!

MADANIKĀ But these jewels belong to my mistress. She left them with Cārudatta for safekeeping!

ŚARVILAKA [*dismayed*] Oh how terrible!

Scorched by the summer sun, I sought a tree
for shelter, and unknowingly stripped it of its leaves.

VASANTASENĀ How remorseful he seems! Obviously he didn't know whom he was robbing.

ŚARVILAKA Madanikā, what's to be done now?

MADANIKĀ You're the one who should know that! You're educated!

ŚARVILAKA That's not the point!

By instinct women know the thing to do,
where men of learning haven't got a clue!

MADANIKĀ All right then! If you take my advice, you'll give the jewels back to the gentleman you stole them from.

ŚARVILAKA But Madanikā! Supposing he takes me to court!

MADANIKĀ I know a bit about Cārudatta. You won't get sunburnt from the moonlight.

VASANTASENĀ Well said, Madanikā! Well said!

ŚARVILAKA All the same, I don't think that would be wise. Have you got any other ideas?

MADANIKĀ Yes, you could take the jewels to my mistress and say that he sent you with them!

ŚARVILAKA And if I do that, what will happen?

MADANIKĀ Well, then you won't be a thief anymore, and Cārudatta will be out of debt, and my mistress will have got her jewels back!

ŚARVILAKA It seems a shame to have to part with them.

MADANIKĀ If you did anything else it would be a shame.

VASANTASENĀ Well said, Madanikā! You talk like a free woman, not a slave!

ŚARVILAKA Through your good counsel, I think I'm finding my conscience, the guide to lead me through the darkest night.

MADANIKĀ Just wait a little while by the shrine of the Love-God, and I'll go and tell my mistress you're here! [*She goes to Vasantasenā.*]

MADANIKĀ Ma'am, there's a Brahman outside who's come from Master Cārudatta.

VASANTASENĀ But Madanikā, how do you know he's from Cārudatta?

MADANIKĀ Why shouldn't I know! He's in love with me!

VASANTASENĀ [*nodding her head and smiling, aside*] Too true! [*aloud*] Bring him in!

ŚARVILAKA [*enters, embarrassed*] Good morning, madam!

VASANTASENĀ Good morning, sir! Please sit down!

ŚARVILAKA Cārudatta the merchant asks me to give you these jewels, and to tell you that he's sending them because his house is in such a state of disrepair that he doesn't feel they're safe there. [*He hands them to Madanikā.*]

VASANTASENĀ Please let me give something in return!

ŚARVILAKA [*aside*] But who's to take it to Cārudatta? I daren't face him. [*aloud*] What may it be, ma'am?

VASANTASENĀ The gift's for you sir! It's Madanikā.

ŚARVILAKA But, lady, I don't understand!

VASANTASENĀ *I* understand. Master Cārudatta asked me to hand over Madanikā to the man who brought back my jewels, and that's just what I'm doing.

ŚARVILAKA [*with great surprise, aside*] It's clear she knows everything! [*aloud*] How generous of Master Cārudatta!

VASANTASENĀ Driver!

[*Driver enters.**]

DRIVER Yes, ma'am, the carriage is ready.

VASANTASENĀ Now, Madanikā, my girl, you're pledged to another, and I have no more control over you. Off you both go in the carriage, and don't forget me.

MADANIKĀ [*weeping*] You're sending me away. [*Falls at Vasantasenā's feet.*]

VASANTASENĀ From now on it's I who should bow to you, a respectable woman! Now off you go!

ŚARVILAKA I thank you, lady! Now Madanikā:

Do as you're told, and say goodbye to her
who's veiled your shady past and made you a wife!

[*Śarvilaka and Madanikā start to leave.*** As they go the voice of the town crier is heard outside.*]

CRIER Attention! Attention!!

ŚARVILAKA [*pausing*] The town crier! [*He holds back Madanikā.*]

CRIER Attention! Attention! The governor proclaims the following instruction. His majesty King Pālaka has been much offended by the rumor that it was prophesied by a soothsayer that the cowherd's son Āryaka would become king. Therefore he has apprehended that traitor and has had him placed in strict confinement! All citizens are commanded to remain in their own districts and to keep the peace.

---

*Original, "with carriage."

**Original, "enter carriage."

ŚARVILAKA [*very excitedly*] Madanikā, that Āryaka is one of my best friends. Now the king's thrown him in jail, and just as we're going to get married! What a dilemma.

Two things are dearest to a man, his friend
and his beloved; but you are safe while he
is in grave danger. So in a case like this
his claim outweighs a hundred lovely women!

So, my darling, I'm not coming!

MADANIKĀ [*weeping and clasping her hands*] Wait, wait a moment! If you must go, at least make sure I'm taken care of while you're away.

ŚARVILAKA Of course, my darling, I was thinking about the same thing! [*to the servant*] My man, do you know where Rebhila the singer lives?

SERVANT Yes, sir.

ŚARVILAKA Then take my lady there.

SERVANT As you say, sir.

MADANIKĀ [*distressed*] I'll do as you say. But please be very careful and come back safe.

[*They go out.*]

ŚARVILAKA Now,

I must find a way to free my friend! [A good job I'm an expert burglar!]
I'll rouse up all my kinsmen, city idlers,
men who have risen in rank by their own endeavor
and court officials who are out of favor. [*Exit.*]

[*Enter slave girl.*]

MAID Madam, a Brahman has come from Master Cārudatta.

VASANTASENĀ Oh, what a lucky day it is! Bring him in, my girl, and show him every respect!

[*The girl goes out and returns with Maitreya.*]

MAID Sir, here is my lady.

MAITREYA Good day, madam!

VASANTASENĀ Greetings, Maitreya. Please sit down.

[*Both sit.*]

VASANTASENĀ And how is the merchant's son?

MAITREYA He's very well, thank you, madam.

VASANTASENĀ
Surely his friends are like the birds who fly
to a fair tree whose buds are virtues, whose trunk
is self-control, whose roots are honesty,
a tree of blessing yielding goodly fruit.

MAITREYA [*aside*] How wickedly charming! She can turn it on, can't she?
[*aloud*] You're quite right, madam.

VASANTASENĀ And what's the reason for your visit, sir?

MAITREYA This, madam! The Lord Cārudatta humbly begs to inform you . . .

VASANTASENĀ [*rises and joins her palms in respect*] What are his orders?

MAITREYA He asks me to tell you that he was foolhardy enough to treat your jewels as though they were his own, and he lost them in gambling. And today he can't find the keeper of the gaming house. He's one of the king's paid informers and he's probably gone to report some information he picked up last night!

VASANTASENĀ [*aside*] He pretends this out of pride. It's things like this that make me love him!

MAITREYA So he asks you to accept this pearl necklace instead [*gives necklace*].

VASANTASENĀ Sir, please tell that gambler Cārudatta I'll call on him this evening.

MAITREYA [*aside*] I wonder what more she's expecting to get from him? [*aloud*] I'll tell him, madam. [*aside*] To keep you at your distance, you harlot! [*Exit.*]

VASANTASENĀ Here, my girl, take the necklace. We'll go and put an end to Cārudatta's miseries.

MAID But look, madam. There's a storm blowing up!

VASANTASENĀ
Let the clouds pile one on another!
Let the rain-filled night loom black!
My heart is fixed on my lover,
and nothing shall turn me back!

# Act V

*Cārudatta's house. Cārudatta, seated, watches the storm outside.*

CĀRUDATTA What an untimely storm! The palace peacocks
fanning their plumage, look up in surprise,
the geese, about to fly to distant lands
hold back in fear, as the sky turns suddenly dark,
clenching the heart of the man sick with longing.
The cloud, black as the wet flank of a buffalo
or a dark bee, garbed in a yellow robe,
of flashing lightning, seems like the great god Viṣṇu,
his conch the skein of storks that crosses the sky.
The rain streams down, from the clouds; its hurrying
silver
drops, for a moment lit by the lamp of lightning,
are like fringes of the garment of the sky.
As a fierce wind tears at the somber clouds,
they paint strange pictures on the sky—great birds
and plunging fish and monsters of the deep
and lofty mansions appear and disappear.

[*thinking*] But it's a long time since Maitreya went to see Vasantasenā, and he still hasn't come back.

[*Enter Maitreya.*]

CĀRUDATTA Why, here he is! Hello, old friend. I'm glad you're back. Please sit down.

MAITREYA I am down—down in the mouth!

CĀRUDATTA Why? What's the cause?

MAITREYA My friend, the cause is lost.

CĀRUDATTA Why? Wouldn't she take the necklace?

MAITREYA No such luck! She reached out her lily-white hand and took it!

CĀRUDATTA Then why did you say our cause is lost?

MAITREYA I should say everything's lost when you give such precious pearls for a box of cheap jewelry that was stolen by a thief before it did us any good. Those pearls were the quintessence of the four oceans.

CĀRUDATTA Oh no, old friend, don't say that!

She put her trust in us by leaving them.
The pearls are a fitting price for her great faith.

MAITREYA And I've got something else to complain about, my friend! When her maid gave a certain sign she put the end of her *sari* over her mouth to hide the fact that she was making fun of me! In my capacity as a Brahman, I respectfully ask you to avoid all further contact with this prostitute.

CĀRUDATTA My friend, I've heard enough of your slanders!

MAITREYA [*aside*] How he rolls his eyes up to the sky and how deeply he sighs! It's clear that his passion is going from bad to worse, and now there's no stopping him!
[*aloud*] Old friend, she asked me to tell you that she was coming to see you this evening. I fancy the necklace of pearls wasn't enough for her and she'll try to get something else out of you!

CĀRUDATTA [*pleased*] How glad I am that she's coming! I'll see to it that she'll be satisfied when she goes.

[*Enter Vasantasenā, very richly dressed, with her face showing signs of longing. With her maid, carrying an umbrella, and a hanger-on—a well-educated young man who has attached himself to her household.*]

HANGER-ON [*announcing Vasantasenā's departure from her house, in mock-pompous verse, like a herald*]

Make way for the Goddess of Fortune without her lotus!
The lovely weapon of the God of Love,
the sorrow of wedded wives, the full-blown flower
of passion's fairest tree. See how alluringly
she walks, yet not lasciviously, restrained
and modest even in ecstasy, she comes
upon the stage of love with all her train.

[*more normal voice*] But hark!

The rolling clouds on the mountain peaks
roar, and the peacocks, frightened by the thunder
flap their wings wildly, like bejeweled fans.
While muddy frogs drink the torrential rain
dark clouds cover the moon and lightning flashes
wildly from one end to another of the sky.

VASANTASENĀ Though the rain pour, though the clouds roar
though thunderbolts fall from above her,
a woman cares nothing for heat or cold
when she goes to meet her lover!

HANGER-ON Fast moving in the tempest
with the torrents of rain like arrows
and thunder like rolling drums
lightning like fluttering banners
the clouds capture the sky
overwhelming the rays of the moon
as an army captures a city.

VASANTASENĀ My heart is in anguish at the mighty clouds
dark as great tuskers, swollen by raging wind,
roaring with thunder, flashing with streaks of
lightning.
The lonely heron calls through the driving rain
and pours a burning acid on my wounds.

HANGER-ON The clouds seem elephants bound by ropes of lightning
bearing away, by order of the Rain God

the earth, with raindrops which
fall like chains of silver.
The land is full of fragrances, and new grass
puts forth its lovely green. The earth is pierced
by jeweled arrows of the pouring rain,
shot by the clouds, whose wings are lightning blown
by mighty winds, as dark as buffalos.
The lotuses are still open-eyed and
it must still be day. In every quarter now
the sky is veiled in darkness, illumined only
by fitful flashes of lightning. Now the world
sleeps motionless within a house of rain
beneath the roof of one tremendous cloud.

VASANTASENĀ The stars have perished like the kindly deed
done to a base man, and the hills are dark
like faces of women who have lost their lovers.
It seems a thunderbolt has struck the heavens
which melt and fall to earth as endless rain.
Then roar, Oh storm-God Indra, pour your rain,
send down your thunderbolts by hundreds! Still
once a woman has set out to meet her lover
you'll never turn her back or break her will.

HANGER-ON The lightning is a golden chain on the rain god's elephant,
it's a pale banner fluttering on a hilltop,
it is the lamp of Indra's heavenly palace,
and it will lead you to your lover's home.

VASANTASENĀ Master, here is the house!

HANGER-ON [*calling loudly*] Hello! Tell this to Master Cārudatta:

Now when the world is perfumed by flowers
opened in the rain, a woman thrilling with love
has reached his home, her tresses wet with rain.
She braved the fear of lightning, rain and thunder
eager to see him. Now she waits outside
washing away the mud from her tinkling anklets.

MAITREYA *[advancing toward her]* Good evening, madam!

VASANTASENĀ Good evening to you, sir. *[to the Hanger-On]* Will you go home now please?

HANGER-ON As you wish, Lady Vasantasenā! *[Exeunt.]*

VASANTASENĀ Master Maitreya! Where's your famous gambler?

MAITREYA He's in the garden, madam, in a rather bad state, I'm afraid. I can't get him to eat or drink. Please come with me!

*[She goes into where Cārudatta is sitting, approaching him from behind so that he does not see her. She plucks a flower and tickles his cheek with it.]*

VASANTASENĀ Are you spending a pleasant evening, you gambler?

CĀRUDATTA *[looks up]* Vasantasenā at last! *[standing up]*

The evenings bring no sleep to me.
I spend the nights in sighs,
but my sorrows end the night I gaze
at my beloved's eyes.

Welcome, my dear lady! Please sit down here!

*[Vasantasenā sits down, followed by the others.]*

CĀRUDATTA I say, Vasantasenā's wet through! Radanikā! *[Enter Radanikā.]* Fetch some dry garments and help the lady change!

RADANIKĀ Certainly, sir, I'm glad to be of service to such a beautiful lady.

*[Vasantasenā goes out with Radanikā and her own maid.]*

MAITREYA *[to Cārudatta]* I say, my friend, I'd like to ask your friend a question.

CĀRUDATTA Go ahead! Here she comes!!

[*Vasantasenā returns wearing dry clothes, with her maid.*]

MAITREYA [*to Vasantasenā, pompously*] Madam, may I respectfully enquire what motive lies behind your visit here on such a miserable evening, when there's no moonlight?

VASANTASENĀ'S MAID [*aside*] I say. He's a stiff-necked old Brahman, right enough!

VASANTASENĀ [*aside*] Yes, he certainly is! You answer him, and be careful what you say!

MAID Sir, my mistress came to ask the value of that pearl necklace.

MAITREYA [*to Cārudatta, aside*] Just what I told you! . . . She isn't satisfied and she's come to ask for more!

MAID You see, she went out gambling last night, and she had the pearl necklace with her. She treated it as though it were her own, and left it as a pledge to pay her gambling debts. The keeper of the gambling house is a government spy, and today he wasn't to be found. Probably he's gone to report something at the palace!

MAITREYA Good Lord! She's saying just what I said!

MAID And until she can see him and redeem the pearls, she wants you to take the golden casket as security.

[*Offers the golden casket.*]

MAITREYA [*surprised*] You look very thoughtful, Cārudatta. Have you seen it before? Why it's the very casket that was stolen from our house!

CĀRUDATTA Yes! It really is the same!

MAID You're right sir, it is!

VASANTASENĀ Master Cārudatta. I'm not worthy to wear these pearls!

MAITREYA [*to Maid*] My dear, are you going to spend the night here?

MAID [*laughing*] Master Maitreya! It's clear you're a *very* strict Brahman.

MAITREYA Old friend, it seems the Rain God has decided to join us again, with some specially large drops! It seems he wants to drive us from this place where we're sitting so comfortably!

CĀRUDATTA
The rain is falling like the pouring of tears
Shed by the clouds in mourning for the moon.

Look, my beloved,

At the evening sky
anointed by the clouds and fanned by cool
and scented breezes. And see! The lightning
comes freely to her lover, who is the sky,
and flings her golden arms about his neck.

[*Vasantasenā registers passionate emotion, and embraces Cārudatta.*]

MAITREYA I'd say the weather is no gentleman, frightening this lady so with the lightning!

CĀRUDATTA
Let it rain for a hundred years,
let the lightning never cease,
now my beloved is by my side
and my heart is at peace!
Happy the man who brings his mistress home
and clasps her close, their bodies cooled by rain.

[*he gazes up*] Look, my darling, a rainbow! Come, let's go in!

Smooth on the palm trees
soft on the bushes
wild on the pools
and harsh on the stones
the rain-drops keep time
like the sound of a lute
plucked by a master
so sweet are their tones.

# Act VI

*A room in Cārudatta's house next morning. Vasantasenā in bed asleep. Enter her maid.*

MAID Wake up, my lady. The sun is rising.

VASANTASENĀ [*waking*] Why! Is it dawn already? And how is your master the gambler today?

MAID He's gone to the Puṣpakaraṇḍa park, ma'am.

VASANTASENĀ Did he leave any instructions?

MAID Yes, ma'am. He said that the carriage was to be got ready for you.

VASANTASENĀ But where am I to go?

MAID To meet him in the park, ma'am.

VASANTASENĀ [*embraces her maid with pleasure*] Marvelous! I didn't think last night that I'd see him today too! Tell me, am I in the inner apartments?

MAID Yes, ma'am; you are in the inner apartments, and in our inmost heart too.

VASANTASENĀ But are Cārudatta's family upset about all this?

MAID They will be ma'am, when you leave them.

VASANTASENĀ My girl, I want you to take this pearl necklace and give it to the Lady Dhūtā. Tell her that I'm the slave of Master Cārudatta, and so I'm her slave too. So the necklace ought to be hers!

MAID But won't Master Cārudatta be annoyed?

VASANTASENĀ Of course not! Take it, now!

MAID Yes, ma'am! [*She takes the necklace. Exit. Soon she returns.*] Madam, the Lady Dhūtā says that her husband made you a present of the necklace, and it wouldn't be right of her to take it back. She said too that you should understand that ornaments didn't matter to her much—because she had one very special ornament, her husband!

[*Enter Radanikā with Rohasena, a small boy, Cārudatta's son.*]

RADANIKĀ Come on, little chap! Let's play with your little cart.

ROHASENA [*whimpering*] Radanikā, I don't like this nasty old clay cart, I want that golden one back!

RADANIKĀ When Daddy's rich again you'll play with a golden cart, dear, but for the time being you'll have to make do with this one. [*seeing Vasantasenā*] Good morning, ma'am!

VASANTASENĀ Good morning, Radanikā! And whose little boy is this? What a sweet little face he has!

RADANIKĀ Why, he's Rohasena, ma'am, Cārudatta's little boy.

VASANTASENĀ [*reaching out her arms*] Come here, darling, let me give you a big hug! [*She takes him on her lap.*] Isn't he the living image of his father!

RADANIKĀ It's not just his face—his personality's like his father's too, and such a great comfort to Master Cārudatta!

VASANTASENĀ But why's he crying?

RADANIKĀ Well, ma'am, you see the little boy who lives opposite has a toy cart all covered with gold, and the other day he came over here to play with Rohasena and brought it with him.

And our boy wanted one like it, but of course we couldn't afford one, so I made the little cart of clay for him. But of course it's a poor substitute!

VASANTASENĀ What a shame! So even a little child is saddened because other children are better off than he is! Fate plays about with men as though they were no more than raindrops on a lotus leaf. [*She wipes a tear.*] There, darling, don't cry! You shall have a golden cart to play with!

ROHASENA Radanikā, who is this lady?

VASANTASENĀ She's the slave of your father, my dear; he won her by his goodness.

RADANIKĀ Darling, this lady is another mother to you!

ROHASENA Silly old Radanikā. If this lady's my mother, why is it she's wearing lots of jewelry?

VASANTASENĀ Oh, you don't know how upsetting the things you say are, you silly little darling! [*She wipes away a tear and takes off her jewels.*] Now I'm really your mother, eh? Take these jewels and Radanikā will get a golden cart made for you with them!

ROHASENA No, I don't want them! I don't want them!

VASANTASENĀ Why not?

ROHASENA Because giving them is making you cry!

VASANTASENĀ [*wiping her tears*] Why, no, my darling, I'm not crying! Now run along and play!

[*She puts her jewels in the little clay cart. Exit Radanikā and Rohasena.*]

[*Enter Vardhamānaka, Cārudatta's servant, driving a covered carriage.*]

VARDHAMĀNAKA [*calling*] Radanikā, Radanikā! Tell the Lady Vasantasenā that the carriage is ready at the side door!

[*Enter Radanikā.*]

RADANIKĀ — Wait a few minutes, Vardhamānaka, while she gets ready!

VARDHAMĀNAKA — All right! While I'm waiting I'll go and get some cushions for the carriage. [*Exits with carriage.*]

[*Enter Sthāvaraka, servant of Saṃsthānaka, driving another carriage.*]

STHĀVARAKA — By Prince Saṃsthānaka's orders I'm off to Puṣpakaraṇḍa Park. [*Cracks whip.*] Get on there, you bullocks! Get on! How the peasant's carts are jamming the road. [*Shouting.*] Out of the way there! Out of the way! This is Prince Saṃsthānaka's carriage, so get out of the way at once! Out of the way you yokels!

VOICE OFF STAGE — I'm stuck! The wheel's come off my cart!! Won't you lend a hand, please?

STHĀVARAKA — What, me? I'll have you know I'm the chief coachman of Prince Saṃsthānaka, and this is his carriage! It's not my job to help country bumpkins in trouble. [*Aside.*] Still, he's a poor man in a lot of trouble—and he can't put the wheel on again without help. It won't take long. I'll leave the carriage outside Cārudatta's side door and go over and give him a hand. [*Exit.*]

RADANIKĀ — I hear the sound of wheels, ma'am. Your carriage is here.

VASANTASENĀ — [*timidly*] My heart's beating so fast, and my right eye's twitching. I wonder if it's a bad omen? [*Enters carriage.*]

[*Enter Sthāvaraka.*]

STHĀVARAKA — That's done! Now I'll get on! Strange how heavy the carriage seems, as though it's loaded. Get on, you lazy bullocks, get on!! [*Exit with carriage containing Vasantasenā.*]

[*Enter the rebel Āryaka, fleeing, a length of chain round one ankle. He pauses, panting, to take a breath.*]

ĀRYAKA — Well, at least I'm out of prison thanks to Śarvilaka the house-breaker but I'm not out of trouble yet by a long shot!

I don't know where I can find shelter. [*looking round*] Here's a broad door, half fallen from its hinges, unbolted, leading to a ruined mansion, whose master must be as unfortunate as I! I'll hide in here!

VARDHAMĀNAKA [*off stage*] Get up there! Get up, you bullock!

ĀRYAKA Oh, a carriage is coming!

[*Enter Vardhamānaka with carriage.*]

VARDHAMĀNAKA I've got the cushions. Radanikā, tell the Lady Vasantasenā the carriage is waiting to take her to the park!

ĀRYAKA It's a courtesan's carriage and it's going out of the town! Just what I was wanting! [*Enters carriage, chain clinking slightly.*]

VARDHAMĀNAKA I can tell she's inside, because I can't hear her anklets tinkling anymore. So I'll be off! Gee up! Gee up!! [*Exit.*]

[*Enter Vīraka, a police guard.*]

VĪRAKA I've put guards on the four gates of the city, now I'll lie in wait for the cowherd's son on top of this heap of rubble. I'll call Candanaka to keep watch with me. [*calling*] Hi! Candanaka! Come over here!

[*Enter Candanaka, a policeman.*]

CANDANAKA Here I am, chief! Any news of the cowherd's son? If we don't catch him the crown will be changing hands. I wonder how he could have got away like that!

[*Enter Vardhamānaka, driving the carriage containing Āryaka.*]

VARDHAMĀNAKA Get on! You lazy bullocks, get on now!

CANDANAKA Look there!

There's an enclosed carriage coming down the high road!
Let's stop it and find out whose it is and where it's going.

VĪRAKA — Halt! Driver, you must tell us whose carriage this is, who's inside it and where it's going!

VARDHAMĀNAKA — All right! It belongs to Master Cārudatta, and I'm taking Lady Vasantasenā to meet him in Puṣpakaraṇḍa Park.

CANDANAKA — [*to Vīraka*] I think we can let it pass!

VĪRAKA — [*to Candanaka*] What! Without searching it?

CANDANAKA — Yes, I'd let it go!

VĪRAKA — Why are you so sure it's all right?

CANDANAKA — Simply because it belongs to Master Cārudatta.

VĪRAKA — But who's this Cārudatta and who's Vasantasenā, that you should trust them so completely?

CANDANAKA — Why, you've not heard of Cārudatta and Vasantasenā! If you've never heard of them you've never heard of the moon in the sky! They are the worthiest people in our city—lovely Vasantasenā and virtuous Cārudatta.

VĪRAKA — Be that as it may! No doubt they're worthy people, but when I'm on duty I don't even know my father.

CANDANAKA — All right! I'll hold the reins while you make a search.

VĪRAKA — No, you look! I'll keep watch.

CANDANAKA — You there, let down the back of the carriage. [*The driver Vardhamānaka does so.*]

ĀRYAKA — [*inside the carriage, aside*] This is a tight corner I'm in! They'll certainly see me and I haven't a weapon of any kind!

> I've still got my two arms! Like ancient heroes
> I'd rather die fighting than go back to prison.
> Still, I may stand a chance if I try another method!

[*Candanaka enters the carriage and sees Āryaka.*]

ĀRYAKA — [*whispering to Candanaka*] I'm at your mercy! I ask your help!

CANDANAKA — [*without looking*] I never refuse my protection.

*[startled, aside, on seeing Āryaka]* Good Lord! It's Āryaka the cowherd's son! I know he's innocent, he's asked my protection, and he's likely to get Cārudatta into trouble if he's caught, since he's riding in his carriage! He's a friend of my good friend Śarvilaka! Yet I'm pledged to the king's service! Whatever can I do! But really, there's no question about it!

He who promises a fugitive protection,
must stand firm by his promise, come what may,
for though he perish, his virtue stays intact.

*[aloud, to Vīraka]* I've inspected the carriage, sir. Master—I mean the Lady Vasantasenā was very annoyed that we stopped her on the way to see Cārudatta.

VĪRAKA Candanaka! There's something fishy about all this.

CANDANAKA Why? What do you suspect?

VĪRAKA You spoke very nervously and you said "Master" and then corrected it to "Lady."

CANDANAKA Oh, but why should you suspect me? You know I'm a southerner and I don't always speak very distinctly. I can speak a bit of about a dozen dialects and languages, but there's no gender in my mother tongue so I often go wrong when I'm speaking other languages.

VĪRAKA Anyway—I'm going to have a look myself. It's the king's orders and I hold a position of trust under the king!

CANDANAKA And don't I hold a position of trust under the king, too?

VĪRAKA Yes, but I'm going to inspect the carriage all the same. The king's orders!

CANDANAKA *[aside]* If he finds Āryaka in Cārudatta's carriage, they'll both be in the soup and me into the bargain! What can I do? I know! I'll start up a quarrel—we southerners are good at that! Hi Vīraka! I, Candanaka, inspected the carriage and now you're going to inspect it again. Who do you think *you* are?

VĪRAKA Who do you think *you* are, giving me orders like that?

CANDANAKA You put on airs and graces and play the gallant officer—but you don't even know your own caste!

VĪRAKA [*angrily*] All right—you tell me then!

CANDANAKA I won't!

VĪRAKA Why not?

CANDANAKA Out of motives of delicacy!

VĪRAKA Enough of that! Driver—turn your carriage! I want to inspect it.

[*Vardhamānaka turns the carriage, and Vīraka goes up to it and begins to mount the steps. As he does so Candanaka seizes him by the hair, drags him to the ground and kicks him.*]

VĪRAKA [*rising, bruised, very angry*] So I'm to be dragged to the ground and kicked while I'm carrying out the king's command, am I? We'll see about that. If I don't have you up before a court martial and torn limb from limb, my name's not Vīraka.

CANDANAKA All right! If that's what you want—off you go to the palace or the nearest police station and inform on me. I'm having no more to do with you, you son of a bitch, or the government you serve.

VĪRAKA That's good enough! I will! [*Exit.*]

CANDANAKA [*looking round apprehensively*] Off you go, coachman! Get on! If you are questioned say that the coach has been searched by the police officers Candanaka and Vīraka and they allowed it to proceed. Lady Vasantasenā, this may serve as a passport for the rest of your journey. [*He hands his sword through the curtains of the coach to Āryaka.*]

ĀRYAKA [*eagerly taking the sword, aside*] Now there's a sword in my right hand I feel as though I'm safe already!

CANDANAKA Lady,

I recognized you and helped you on your way.
Remember Candanaka when you reach your goal.
Not out of greed I ask, but out of love.

ĀRYAKA You risked your life to help me in my need,
So now, brave Candanaka, you're my friend,
through a strange fate. And if the prophecy
comes true, I will reward you in the end.

CANDANAKA May Śiva, Viṣṇu, Brahmā, Sun and Moon
guard you in every peril and keep you safe.

[*Vardhamānaka drives off with the carriage containing Āryaka.*]

CANDANAKA [*watching him go*] Well, this isn't a very healthy city to live in now that my old boss Captain Vīraka is out for my blood. I'll go home quickly and round up all the men of the family, and we'll all be off to join Śarvilaka and the rest of the rebels.

# Act VII

*Puṣpakaraṇḍa Park, the same morning. Enter Cārudatta and Maitreya.*

MAITREYA How lovely the park looks this morning!

CĀRUDATTA It certainly does!

It's like a multicolored market where
the trees are merchants and the flowers their wares,
while the bees are tax collectors levying
from stall to stall their fragrant market dues.

MAITREYA Let's sit on this slab of natural rock. It looks very charming.

CĀRUDATTA [*sits*] Vardhamānaka's a long time, isn't he?

MAITREYA He told me that he'd drive slowly so as not to shake her up.

[*Enter Vardhamānaka, driving the carriage in which Āryaka is concealed.*]

VARDHAMĀNAKA Get up, you bullocks! Get along there!

ĀRYAKA [*aside*]

Afraid lest the king's henchmen see me, still
wearing this length of chain that slows my flight—
here I am, hidden in a good man's carriage,
a cuckoo, nourished in a raven's nest.

Well, I'm outside the city, anyway. Shall I jump out and hide in the thick undergrowth or shall I wait and see the carriage's owner? That's what I'll do! It's said that Cārudatta always helps people in trouble and I don't think he'll let me down.

VARDHAMĀNAKA Well, here's the park! [*He halts the carriage, gets down, and goes up to Maitreya.*] Master Maitreya!

MAITREYA [*to Cārudatta*] My friend, Vasantasenā's here at last! [*to Vardhamānaka*] You son of a servant girl, why have you been so long?

VARDHAMĀNAKA Please don't be so angry, Master Maitreya! I forgot the cushions for the carriage and I had to go back for them!

CĀRUDATTA Maitreya, my friend, help Vasantasenā down!

MAITREYA One would think she had chains on her feet, since it seems she can't get down herself! [*Gets up and looks into carriage.*] Good Lord! It's not Vasantasenā, or if it is she's changed her sex!

CĀRUDATTA Really old man, this isn't the time for jokes! Love can't wait, you know. I'll help her down myself. [*Gets up and goes over to carriage.*]

ĀRYAKA [*watching him approach*] So this is the owner of the carriage. He looks just as handsome and kindly as his reputation. I'm sure he'll help me.

CĀRUDATTA [*looking into the carriage*] I say! Whoever's this?

His arms are thick as trunks of elephants,
his shoulders wide and muscled like a lion's.
How broad his chest! How dark his rolling eyes!
A chain trails from his ankle. How can it be
that one so noble of bearing should bear such ignominy?

Who are you, sir?

ĀRYAKA I am Āryaka the cowherd's son! I ask your protection!

CĀRUDATTA The man who was captured by King Pālaka on account of a silly rumor.

ĀRYAKA Yes, that's me!

CĀRUDATTA

Destiny has brought you to me. I am true
to my resolves, and I would rather give
my life up than I'd give up you, my friend.

*[Āryaka registers relief and pleasure.]*

CĀRUDATTA *[to Vardhamānaka]* Vardhamānaka, get that chain off his leg!

VARDHAMĀNAKA I will, sir! *[Does so, taking file from carriage.]* There you are! It's done!

ĀRYAKA From now on I'm chained by even stronger fetters—by bonds of affection to you, Master Cārudatta.

MAITREYA Yes, now he's free of his chains! It won't be long now before we'll be wearing them, if I'm not mistaken!

CĀRUDATTA You ought to be ashamed of yourself Maitreya! Stop complaining!

ĀRYAKA I thank you, friend Cārudatta, for the use of your carriage, and I beg your pardon for taking a lift in it without your consent. Now with your permission, I think I ought to go! *[He starts to alight from the carriage.]*

CĀRUDATTA No! Don't get down, my friend. You're a man who's easily recognized wherever you go, and there are always lots of people around this park. They'll take no notice of a covered carriage. So I think you'd better stop where you are.

ĀRYAKA You're really most kind, sir!

CĀRUDATTA Now go in safety to your friend.

ĀRYAKA Henceforth you are among the dearest friends I have.

CĀRUDATTA Remember me in happier times.

ĀRYAKA I will, as I remember my own self.

CĀRUDATTA May the gods protect you on your way!

ĀRYAKA As you today have so well protected me!

CĀRUDATTA It was good fortune that kept you safe.

ĀRYAKA But you were my good fortune.

CĀRUDATTA Now King Pālaka's men will be on your heels. You'd better be going right away!

ĀRYAKA All right! I'll see you again! [*Exit in carriage.*]

CĀRUDATTA

Now I have aided the king's enemies!
We mustn't stay a moment longer here.
Maitreya! Throw the chain into that old well.
King's eyes see everywhere through secret agents.

[*He rubs his left eye.*] Friend Maitreya! How badly I want to see Vasantasenā!

I haven't seen her today and my left eye twitches,
my heart is palpitating as though from fear!

Let's go! Look—there's a Buddhist monk down the road! Another bad omen! Let's leave by the other way so as not to meet him. [*Exeunt.*]

# Act VIII

*The same scene. Enter Saṃvāhaka, now a Buddhist monk, carrying a monk's robe.*

SAṂVĀHAKA [*apparently addresses the audience*] Sirs, we should gather merit!

Control your appetites, and through the drum
of meditation always keep awake,
for those slick thieves, the senses, are out to steal
the virtue gained in the course of many lives.

All things must pass away, and therefore I find refuge in the Law of Righteousness! However, I must wash my robe, for the master taught us to keep our clothes clean as well as our minds. So I'll do it in the lotus pool in the park. It's not far away.

[*He crosses the stage and kneels by the pool.*]

SAṂSTHĀNAKA [*off stage*] Stop, you rascally beggar. Stop!

SAṂVĀHAKA [*alarmed*] Oh dear! Here comes Saṃsthānaka, the king's brother-in-law. Once a Buddhist monk stood up to him and told him what he thought of him and since then he hates us all and persecutes every monk he finds. Where can I hide? [*Pulls himself together.*] The Lord Buddha will be my refuge.

[*Enter Saṃsthānaka, with Viṭa, who wears a sword.*]

SAṂSTHĀNAKA Stop, you vile beggar, stop, so that I can smash your ugly head, that's as bald as a turnip. [*Strikes him.*]

VIṬA You know you ought not to strike a monk, you silly bastard! What's the point anyway, when we can enjoy ourselves in the park. Look, sir:

> The trees perform deeds of kindness, giving shade
> and rest to men lonely and travel-worn.
> No violence is needed to enjoy
> this park, a new kingdom completely undefended.

SAṂVĀHAKA [*very calmly*] Welcome, my son! Be calm, my son, you servant of the Lord.

SAṂSTHĀNAKA Listen to him! He's insulting me.

VIṬA How?

SAṂSTHĀNAKA He's calling me a servant. I'm not the Lord's servant, I'm the Lord's brother-in-law.

VIṬA He doesn't mean the king, you fool, he means the Lord Buddha. He's paying you a compliment.

SAṂSTHĀNAKA Go on then, you dirty monk, pay me some more.

SAṂVĀHAKA My son, if only you would see clearly, you are already holy, you enjoy the glory of the divine right, you possess the blessed state Nirvāṇa already.*

SAṂSTHĀNAKA What rubbish he's talking! I'm not the king though I may be his brother-in-law. *I* don't enjoy any divine right! And as for the state of Nirvāṇa I've never heard of the place, and even if it does exist I certainly don't possess it. The man's crazy! Why's he here anyway?

SAṂVĀHAKA I came to wash my robe.

SAṂSTHĀNAKA You filthy beggar! This is the finest park in the neighborhood and was given to me by my sister's husband the king!

* This and the next speech inserted by A.L.B. to replace untranslatable and obscure word plays in the original.

Why, the jackals drink out of the pond, and even I, the best man in the city, won't bathe in it. And here you come and defile it by washing your filthy stinking yellow robe in it! Now I'll kill you with one blow. [*Strikes Saṃvāhaka.*]

SAṂVĀHAKA [*keeping calm with evident difficulty*] Praise be to the Lord Buddha!

VIṬA [*angrily*] Why must you hit the poor chap? Let him go!

SAṂSTHĀNAKA I'll think it over, and see how my heart feels about it.

VIṬA [*aside*] Why doesn't the monk go away while the going's good?

SAṂSTHĀNAKA [*aside*] Now, my dear little heart, what shall we do about this monk here. Shall he go or shall he stay or shall he do neither?
[*aloud*] I've talked it over with my heart and this is what my heart says.

VIṬA What does it say?

SAṂSTHĀNAKA He shan't go and he shan't stay. He shan't breathe in and he shan't breathe out. He shall die this instant.

SAṂVĀHAKA [*calmly*] Praise be to the Buddha! In him I take refuge!!

VIṬA Let him go, now.

SAṂSTHĀNAKA All right, but on one condition.

VIṬA What's that?

SAṂSTHĀNAKA [*laughing at his own joke*] Either he must take a handful of mud out of the bottom of the pool without dirtying the water, or he must pick up a handful of water, roll it into a ball, and throw it on the ground!

VIṬA [*aside*] He's absolutely crazy!

[*Saṃvāhaka the monk loses his self-control sufficiently to give Saṃsthānaka a glance conveying extreme contempt, and walks off with dignity.*]

VIṬA [*to Saṃsthānaka*] Now he's gone! Why not put him out of your mind and enjoy this beautiful park?

SAṂSTHĀNAKA Yes, that's a good idea! It really is nice, isn't it. It reminds me of a lovely poem—did I ever recite it to you? I composed it myself:

The earth is clad with lots of pretty flowers.
The blooming trees are standing stiff as flunkeys,
while far above us, like big round breadfruit fruits,
hang from the treetops hordes of chattering monkeys!

Rather good, don't you think? It's not every poet could think of a rhyme for monkeys!*

VIṬA [*bored*] Come and sit down on this rock, you silly bastard!

SAṂSTHĀNAKA All right! [*They sit.*] You know, even now I can't get Vasantasenā out of my mind! It's like when some low type insults you—you just can't forget it!

VIṬA [*aside*]

Disdain inflames the passions of
the coward and the fool,
But the man of taste and breeding,
disdained, himself turns cool.

SAṂSTHĀNAKA I say, what's the time? I told Sthāvaraka to bring the carriage and he's still not here. I'm getting hungry! And now it's midday and too hot to go home on foot!

VIṬA You're right.

The cows sleep in the shade, too tired to chew the cud
the forest deer drink at the half-dry pool
and slake their burning thirst with sun-warmed water.
No traveler ventures on the highway now.
The carriage pauses to shelter from the sun.

SAṂSTHĀNAKA Now the sun sits, his feet upon my head,
the birds, the fowls of air, sit on the trees.

---

* Alas, this last remark isn't in the original, but the verse (originally unrhymed) is not too far off!

Humans and men are panting from the heat,
and only sitting in the shelter of their homes do they find ease.

That wasn't bad, either, was it? And still the carriage doesn't come! I think I'll sing a little, to pass the time. Have you ever heard me sing, by the way?

VIṬA [*not paying attention*] What were you saying? Oh yes, you sing like an angel!

SAṂSTHĀNAKA Yes, I know I do! Eating hot spices and roast cuckoos! That's the secret of a good voice. Now I'll give you a real treat. [*He clears this throat and prepares to sing.*]

VIṬA [*hurriedly*] It's all right sir. I hear the carriage coming.

[*Enter Sthāvaraka, Saṃsthānaka's coachman, with the carriage containing Vasantasenā.*]

STHĀVARAKA How hot the midday sun is! I'm afraid Saṃsthānaka will be cranky with me so I'd better hurry. Get on, you bullocks, get on!

VASANTASENĀ [*in the carriage*] That wasn't Vardhamānaka's voice! Whatever can have happened? Maybe Cārudatta sent another carriage and driver.

SAṂSTHĀNAKA Ah, now I can hear the carriage! It's grunting like an old pig.

[*Sthāvaraka pulls up the carriage at a point some distance away, representing the other side of the park wall.*]

SAṂSTHĀNAKA [*calls*] Sthāvaraka, my boy! Are you there?

STHĀVARAKA Yes, sir!

SAṂSTHĀNAKA And is the carriage there?

STHĀVARAKA Yes, sir!

SAṂSTHĀNAKA And are the bullocks there?

STHĀVARAKA Yes, sir!

SAṂSTHĀNAKA And are you there?

STHĀVARAKA [*irritated*] My Lord! I too am here!

SAṂSTHĀNAKA Then bring the carriage into the park.

STHĀVARAKA Which way shall I bring it?

SAṂSTHĀNAKA Right here, where the wall is broken down.

STHĀVARAKA But sir, if I try to drive the carriage over that heap of bricks in this heat, it will kill the bullocks and break up the carriage—and probably I'll die of heatstroke into the bargain.

SAṂSTHĀNAKA My man, I'll have you know that I'm the king's brother-in-law. If the bullocks die I'll get two more. If the carriage is smashed I'll have another one made. And if you die I'll soon get another driver!

STHĀVARAKA Yes, it's all right as far as you're concerned. But where would I get a replacement for myself?

SAṂSTHĀNAKA Stop grumbling! I don't care if the bullocks and the carriage and you too all fall to pieces! I want the carriage driven through that gap in the wall!

STHĀVARAKA [*aside*] All right—let the carriage smash—along with its owner. He'll have to get another one. I'll report this to His Majesty when I get back.

[*He drives through the gap in the wall. Vasantasenā inside the carriage is badly shaken up and registers great alarm.*]

STHĀVARAKA [*aside, sighing with relief*] Well, I've made it!
[*aloud*] Sir, here is your carriage!

SAṂSTHĀNAKA You see the bullocks aren't broken and the carriage isn't dead!

STHĀVARAKA No, sir.

SAṂSTHĀNAKA [*pompously*] Now, Viṭa, you are my teacher, my chief preceptor. And seeing that you are such a worthy, honorable and highly polished gentleman, I graciously bestow on you the honor of entering the carriage first.

VIṬA Just as you like. [*Starts to enter.*]

SAṂSTHĀNAKA But wait a moment! Is it your family carriage or is it mine? I'm the owner, so I've decided that I'll get in first.

VIṬA [*irritated*] Just as you say!

SAṂSTHĀNAKA [*on his dignity*] You have committed a breach of etiquette. You should have said "pray mount your carriage, my lord!"

VIṬA [*impatiently*] All right, get in!

STHĀVARAKA [*as Saṃsthānaka walks towards carriage, bowing*] Pray mount your carriage, my lord.

SAṂSTHĀNAKA [*glances approvingly at Sthāvaraka as he mounts the carriage; looks in and hurries away again in great fear.*] Oh, I'm dying, I'm dying! There's something in there. It's either a she-demon or a thief, I don't know which. If it's a she-demon she'll rob us both and if it's a thief she'll eat us both.

VIṬA I'm sure there's nothing to be so scared about. Whoever heard of a demon taking a ride in a bullock carriage in broad daylight? You were just dazzled by the bright sunlight, and when you looked into the carriage you saw Sthāvaraka's shadow on the carriage curtain.

SAṂSTHĀNAKA But I'm sure I saw a woman there, in the back of the carriage. You look for yourself!

VIṬA What! A woman!

VASANTASENĀ [*very alarmed, aside*] The king's brother-in-law, that eyesore! I'm afraid he'll recognize me. Whatever can I do?

SAṂSTHĀNAKA That cowardly driver won't look in. You go and see what's there.

VIṬA All right! I'm not scared. [*He looks in.*] Why, it's simply impossible. The deer has come to the tiger! I'm really sorry!

The swan has left her mate
as white as the moon, to go
to the bank of another river
with a common crow!

[*whispering to Vasantasenā*] Vasantasenā, you shouldn't have come here. It isn't like you to come here.

At first you sent back the money
he'd touched with his dirty paws.
But a certain lack of self-respect
is the nature of common whores!
But I suppose your mother made you come.

And anyway, Vasantasenā, who am I to lay down the law? I remember only the other day I told you that when a courtesan started to pick and choose she was losing her grip.

VASANTASENĀ It's all a mistake! I got into the wrong carriage! I'm at your mercy!

VIṬA [*changes tone*] I see! I'm sorry I didn't realize what had happened! There, don't be afraid. I'll fool him. [*aloud, to Saṃsthānaka*] There really is a she-demon in there!

SAṂSTHĀNAKA Then why didn't she rob you, or if it's a thief, why didn't she eat you?

VIṬA Anyway, it seems there's something unpleasant about the carriage. Why don't we let the bullocks have a rest, and walk home. It's a bit cooler now.

SAṂSTHĀNAKA All right! Sthāvaraka—rest the bullocks and bring the carriage back later. Wait, though! No! I've changed my mind! *I* walk only in the presence of gods and Brahmans. No, we'll go in the carriage after all! Then the people will know that the Lord Saṃsthānaka, brother-in-law of the king, is on the way.

VIṬA [*aside*] It's not easy to change poison into medicine, but I'll do my best!
[*aloud*] Actually I was only joking! In fact it's Vasantasenā in the carriage. She's come to see you!

VASANTASENĀ [*aside*] Heaven forbid that I should ever come to see him!

SAṂSTHĀNAKA [*very pleased*] Marvelous! She's come to see me, a superhuman human being, no ordinary mortal.

VIṬA Of course.

SAṂSTHĀNAKA Most exceptional good luck! She was really angry with me, and now I'll fall at her feet and beg her pardon.

VIṬA Yes, that's just what you ought to do.

SAṂSTHĀNAKA [*goes up to Vasantasenā*] I humbly fall at your feet and beg your pardon, my goddess! Listen to what I say:

Oh large-eyed lady, I fall before your feet
with their full complement of ten toenails, I crave
pardon with joined palms for the wrong I did you.
Forgive me, white-toothed lady; I'm your slave!

VASANTASENĀ [*angrily*] Go away. I won't lower myself by giving in to you! [*She kicks his head with her foot.*]

SAṂSTHĀNAKA [*angrily*]

This head, which my mother and my granny
kissed with such love; this head which even to the
gods
never bowed in reverence; this noble head
is struck by a harlot's foot, like a dead skull
kicked by a jackal running in the forest.

Sthāvaraka, where did you pick her up?

STHĀVARAKA The road was blocked by the peasant's wagons, sir, and I stopped the carriage outside Cārudatta's garden to help a man whose wheel had come off. I fancy she got in by mistake while the carriage was waiting.

SAṂSTHĀNAKA Oh, so she's come by mistake! Then get out of my carriage! Get out of it! You wanted to come here to meet that poverty-stricken son of a merchant, you slut, and you came in my carriage. Get out of it!

VASANTASENĀ [*sighing*] Very well! What is to be, will be.

SAṂSTHĀNAKA
With these two hands, adorned with finger nails,
as good at fondling as they are at fighting,
I'll drag you from my carriage by the hair,
my slender beauty, and throw you to the ground.

VIṬA It's not decent to drag a woman like that by the hair. Wait a minute. I'll see that she comes out. Vasantasenā, please get down. [*Gives her his hand.*]

[*Vasantasenā gets down from carriage and stands on one side.*]

SAṂSTHĀNAKA [*aside*]

Now that she's again treated me so vilely I feel angrier than ever. She has fanned the flames of my wrath, and since she kicked me they're raging even more fiercely. I'll kill her, that's what I'll do!

[*aloud to Viṭa, in a wheedling tone*] Viṭa,

what about a fine new cloak with a long fringe,
embroidered with hundreds of different colors?
And wouldn't you like to eat your fill of all sorts of meat?

VIṬA What's behind all this?

SAṂSTHĀNAKA I want you to do me a favor.

VIṬA I'll do anything you want, as long as it's honest.

SAṂSTHĀNAKA I swear there's not even the smell of dishonesty about it. It's all perfectly straightforward.

VIṬA Well, then, what is it?

SAṂSTHĀNAKA Kill Vasantasenā!

VIṬA [*with a gesture of horror*]

This lovely lady is our city's pride.
Though she's a courtesan, she's capable
of great affection and true nobility.
She's done no wrong, and if I were to kill her
no bark would bear me over death's dark river
to find a happy birth in the life to come.

SAṂSTHĀNAKA Don't let that worry you! I'll buy you a boat! And anyway, there's no one about in this lonely park. Who'd see you if you killed her?

VIṬA
All the directions of endless space would see me.
The wood-nymphs and the hot-rayed sun would see me.
The wind would see me, and the heaven and earth
would see me. My inmost soul would see me.
The infinite Spirit of Righteousness would see me.
These are all witnesses of good and evil.

SAṂSTHĀNAKA Well, cover her up with your cloak, and then you can kill her.

VIṬA You fool! You low, immoral fool!!

SAṂSTHĀNAKA [*aside*] The fellow's too scrupulous. All right, I'll try Sthāvaraka!
[*aloud*] Sthāvaraka, my boy—would you like me to give you some bracelets?

STHĀVARAKA Yes, I'd love to wear them.

SAṂSTHĀNAKA *And* I'll have a chair covered with gold made specially for you.

STHĀVARAKA It would be really nice to sit on a gold chair!

SAṂSTHĀNAKA *And* I'll see that you're always given all the left-over food from my table.

STHĀVARAKA The thought of it makes my mouth water.

SAṂSTHĀNAKA *And* I'll put you in charge of my domestic staff.

STHĀVARAKA I'll keep them in order, sir!

SAṂSTHĀNAKA Then you must do what I tell you.

STHĀVARAKA I'll do anything you tell me, sir, as long as it's honest.

SAṂSTHĀNAKA Oh! What I want you to do is perfectly honest!

STHĀVARAKA Then tell me what it is, sir!

SAṂSTHĀNAKA Kill that Vasantasenā!

STHĀVARAKA [*very nervously*] Please, master, don't be angry. I'm only a common man, and I was responsible for the lady mistaking her carriage and coming here. I can't do her any more harm!

SAṂSTHĀNAKA [*angry*] Why, you're only a common servant, and it seems I've no power even over you.

STHĀVARAKA You've power over my body, master, but not over my mind, when it comes to the question of what's right and wrong. Please don't be angry, master, I just can't do it! Oh, how frightened I am!

SAṂSTHĀNAKA You're my slave! What have you got to be afraid of?

STHĀVARAKA I'm afraid for my state in the next world, master!

SAṂSTHĀNAKA And what's the next world you're so worried about?

STHĀVARAKA It's the ripening of one's good and evil deeds.

SAṂSTHĀNAKA And what's the ripening of good deeds?

STHĀVARAKA To live in luxury, just like you do, sir!

SAṂSTHĀNAKA And of bad deeds?

STHĀVARAKA To become a miserable ghost, with nothing to eat but scraps left from offerings made to other dead men.

SAṂSTHĀNAKA So you won't kill her then, you superstitious fool. [*Beats him mercilessly.*]

STHĀVARAKA Beat me, master, kill me if you like. I won't do such a wicked deed.

I was born a slave. Destiny willed it thus
for sins committed in a former life.
I will earn no more misery, and so
I shun all crime, and strive to do men good.

VIṬA Stop it, you bastard! Have pity on him! [*aside*] Well done, Sthāvaraka, well done!

This poor and lowly servant, the tool of others,
unlike his master, strives for righteousness.
Why is it that men do not promptly perish
when they abandon decency and augment evil?

SAṂSTHĀNAKA [*aside*] The old jackal is afraid of losing merit and the slave is afraid of a next world. But I'm the king's brother-in-law. I'm no ordinary man. What have I got to be afraid of? [*aloud*] You go home, you lowborn slave, and wait for me there.

STHĀVARAKA As you wish, sir. [*to Vasantasenā*] Lady, I can't do any more to help you.

SAṂSTHĀNAKA [*tightens his belt*] Wait a minute, Vasantasenā! I'm just coming over there to kill you.

VIṬA You won't kill her while I'm here!

[*He seizes Saṃsthānaka by the throat. Saṃsthānaka pretends to faint, and watches Viṭa make signs to Vasantasenā to escape. He pretends to regain consciousness.*]

SAṂSTHĀNAKA [*aside*] The old jackal. I've fed him all these years and now in my greatest need he's turned against me. I'll have to get him out of the way somehow before I can kill Vasantasenā. [*aloud, to Viṭa*] Sir, you took me too seriously. I'm a man of enormously noble birth—how could I do anything really wicked? I only said what I did because I thought she might give in.

VIṬA

Your birth is quite irrelevant—
a man's known by his deeds.
And it's the richest cornfield
that grows rankest weeds.

SAṂSTHĀNAKA Look, I've no intention of harming her. I know she'd like to give in to me really, but when you're here she's ashamed to do so, because you've heard that she won't. Now, you go away for a bit. I've beaten that slave Sthāvaraka so badly that I'm sure he'll try to run away. So please go after him and try to find him and bring him back.

VIṬA [*aside*] Maybe he's right. She really did come here to see Saṃsthānaka, but she has to put on this act because I'm about.
[*aloud*] All right, I'll go.

VASANTASENĀ [*grasping the ends of his robe*] Don't go! I put myself in your care!

VIṬA There's nothing to fear now, Vasantasenā. Saṃsthānaka, I trust you to take good care of her! You're responsible for her safety.

SAṂSTHĀNAKA Don't worry. She's quite safe in my hands.

VIṬA You swear it?

SAṂSTHĀNAKA I swear it!

VIṬA [*after going some distance*] But he's so cruel and treacherous I can't trust him not to kill her. Perhaps I'd better hide and watch what he gets up to! [*Does so.*]

SAṂSTHĀNAKA [*aside*] Now's my chance. I'll kill her right enough this time! But how can I be sure the wily old fox isn't hiding somewhere, to see what I do? I'd better try to fool him! [*aloud, as he plucks flowers*] Dear little Vasantasenā, please come over here!

VIṬA Why—he's in love with her again! There's evidently no need to worry now, so I'll be off!

SAṂSTHĀNAKA
I offer gold, I speak kind loving words,
I lay my turbaned head beneath your feet
and yet you still reject me. White-toothed lady,
why do you only give your love to beggars?

VASANTASENĀ You rogue, you base-born cherub, why do you try
to win my favors with your wealth? The bees
will not forsake the pure immaculate lotus.
One should serve the man of honor, though he be poor.
To love such men is glorious, even in courtesans.

SAṂSTHĀNAKA You low slut! Will you never leave off insulting me? Will you never forget that Cārudatta?

VASANTASENĀ He is in my heart, so how can I ever forget him?

SAṂSTHĀNAKA I'll show you how! I'll kill you right now, and then I'll go and kill him, too. Let that son of a whore the poverty-stricken Cārudatta protect you now, if he can.

VASANTASENĀ He'd save me if he could.

SAṂSTHĀNAKA Oh no! Not all the gods and heroes could save you now. I'm really going to kill you!

VASANTASENĀ Oh Cārudatta! I die full of love for you, Cārudatta!!

SAṂSTHĀNAKA The whore still calls his name! [*He seizes her by the throat.*] Remember him, you slut, remember him well, for you won't remember him much longer.

VASANTASENĀ [*choking*] Cārudatta!

SAṂSTHĀNAKA Die, you harlot! Die!! [*His grip tightens on her throat and she falls motionless to the ground.*]

SAṂSTHĀNAKA [*joyfully*]

That sink of vice, that vile and cheating slut
lies dead through the valor of a hero's hand,
the hero being me. She would not have me
though I desired her. So the whore lies dead!

[*Looks round.*] But here's the old jackal coming back! I'd better hide the body. [*Does so.*]

[*Re-enter Viṭa with Sthāvaraka.*]

VIṬA — [*as he walks*] How terrible! A tree fell across the road and killed a poor woman. We must report this accident when we return. It's a bad omen, too. A dead woman? I wonder what that bastard has been up to with Vasantasenā. I pray that the gods will guard her from harm. [*Goes up to Saṃsthānaka.*] Here we are! I found Sthāvaraka and brought him back.

SAṂSTHĀNAKA — Welcome, Viṭa. And welcome, Sthāvaraka, my boy.

STHĀVARAKA — As you say, sir!

VIṬA — What about the lady I left in your care?

SAṂSTHĀNAKA — What lady?

VIṬA — Vasantasenā.

SAṂSTHĀNAKA — She's gone.

VIṬA — Where?

SAṂSTHĀNAKA — The way you came.

VIṬA — Then why didn't we meet her? There's something fishy about all this. Now tell me the truth.

SAṂSTHĀNAKA — I swear by your head and my own feet—I've killed her.

VIṬA — [*very perturbed*] What! You've killed her?

SAṂSTHĀNAKA — If you don't believe the word of the king's brother-in-law, look yourself. [*Shows Vasantasenā's body.*] There's the result of my heroism!

VIṬA — [*in great distress*] Horrible! I'm to blame—I shouldn't have left her with the brute!

STHĀVARAKA — Oh no, sir! it's not your fault. I'm the one who's really to blame because I should have realized that she was in the carriage.

VIṬA — [*in tears*]

The river of grace runs dry.
The Goddess of Love has fled.
The jewel among women,
the fount of joy, lies dead.
So kind and so gentle,
the friend of such as I,
she may have sold her beauty,
her soul no man could buy!

[*to Saṃsthānaka in great anger*] You vile madman, you're evil itself incarnate. Why did you kill this harmless woman, the most beautiful woman in town?
[*aside*] Very likely he'll try to lay the blame on me. I'd better go. [*Starts walking off. Saṃsthānaka runs after him and tries to hold him back.*]

VIṬA Don't touch me, you vile creature, don't touch me. I've finished with you. Let me go!

SAṂSTHĀNAKA You've killed Vasantasenā yourself, and now you're trying to lay the blame on me! Where do you think you can hide?

VIṬA You can't get away with that one, you reprobate. There's a witness you know.

SAṂSTHĀNAKA I'll give a hundred gold pieces if you'll help me to keep this quiet.

VIṬA Let me go! You can keep your money!

STHĀVARAKA May heaven have mercy on us!

[*Saṃsthānaka smiles at Viṭa and pretends affection.*]

VIṬA All right then, smile. But we are enemies henceforward. Shame on friendship with a scorned and baseborn coward. I won't see you again. I throw you aside like a broken, stringless bow.

SAṂSTHĀNAKA Please come back, good sir. Please! Look, let's go and bathe in the pond.

VIṬA If I associate with you I'll lose my honor completely, and people will think I was your accomplice in crime. How can I remain a useless hanger-on of a man who murders women?

Lovely Vasantasenā, may you never
again be born a courtesan, but become
in your next incarnation a noble lady,
mother of sons, the darling of her husband.

SAṂSTHĀNAKA You've killed Vasantasenā in my park and now you're trying to escape and throw the blame on me! You're a murderer. [*Places his hand on Viṭa's shoulder.*] I arrest you! You shall be tried before my brother-in-law the king!

VIṬA [*whipping out his sword*] Is that so? Get back, you brute!

SAṂSTHĀNAKA [*retreating, frightened*] Why, you're so frightened! All right, I'll let you go!

VIṬA [*aside*] It won't do to stay here! My place is with my friends Śarvilaka and Candanaka, with the rebels! [*Exit.*]

SAṂSTHĀNAKA Go to hell, then! Now Sthāvaraka, what have I done?

STHĀVARAKA I'm afraid you've committed a great sin, sir.

SAṂSTHĀNAKA [*angrily*] What! You, a servant, have the audacity to accuse me of sin? [*calmer*] Well, we'll say no more about it. [*Offers a jewel.*] Look, this is yours! I give it to you, and in future every time I put on my jewels I'll give one to you.

STHĀVARAKA But things like that aren't in my line, sir. What use has a poor man like me for jewelry?

SAṂSTHĀNAKA [*annoyed and nervous*] Very well, then. Take the bullocks back to the palace and wait there till I come home!

STHĀVARAKA As you say, sir. [*Exit.*]

SAṂSTHĀNAKA Now Viṭa's cleared off for his own safety, and there's nothing I can do about it. But I'll take care to have that driver kept in chains in the palace tower, so as to make sure he keeps his mouth shut. First, though, I'd better see that she's quite dead. If she isn't I'll have to kill her over again!

Yes, she's well and truly dead. I'll cover her with my cloak. No, I'd better not, it's marked with my name. I'll cover her with a heap of dead leaves, that's a better idea! [*Does so.*] There! That's done! Now I'll go to the court and make a formal accusation against Cārudatta. I'll declare that he came to Puṣpakaraṇḍa Park, which is my property, and murdered Vasantasenā to get her jewelry. Ha! Ha!

To ruin Cārudatta
I've a new trick in my box!
To keep our noble city clean,
they'll kill him like an ox.

So here I go! [*Looks around, suddenly registers alarm.*] Oh, no! Wherever I go, I'm always running into that blasted monk! Here he comes again, still carrying his filthy robe! He mustn't see me here or he'll tell everyone I killed Vasantasenā. I'd better get away through the gap in the wall. [*Exit.*]

[*Enter the monk Saṃvāhaka.*]

SAṂVĀHAKA I've washed my robe, so now I'll hang it on a branch to dry. No, I'd better not, there are too many monkeys about and the ground's too dusty. I know, I'll spread it out on that heap of dead leaves over there, and I'll meditate while it's drying. [*Spreads the robe and sits cross-legged muttering Buddhist liturgy.*] Glory be to the Lord Buddha, the all-worthy, the fully enlightened.

I go for refuge to the Buddha
I go for refuge to the Doctrine
I go for refuge to the Order.
May I be peaceful
May I be kindly
May I be unharmed
May I keep my inner happiness
And even as I
May all living things be peaceful
May they be kindly,
May they be unharmed,
May they . . . [*sighs*]

Oh, it's no good. I'm a poor kind of a monk, I'm afraid. I can't concentrate for ten seconds on end. I just can't get the Lady Vasantasenā out of my mind, because she was so good to me. It was she who rescued me from the clutches of gambling with the ten gold pieces which paid my debts. Surely she is the servant of the Lord Buddha without knowing it, despite her profession. Ever since then I've felt in a sense her slave. I wish I could pay her back. The Lord Buddha said the most precious gift was the gift of the true Doctrine. Perhaps one day I'll be able to set her on the road to Nirvāṇa. But's what's that sighing voice coming from under those leaves?

[*Vasantasenā's arm emerges from the heap of dead leaves.*]

SAṂVĀHAKA Why! It's a woman's arm, all covered with jewels! And another. I think I recognize them! They are surely the very hands which saved me from misery! [*Removes leaves.*] Yes, it's the servant of the Lord Buddha, the Lady Vasantasenā. [*He fans her with the end of his robe to her senses.*]

VASANTASENĀ Who are you, sir?

SAṂVĀHAKA Don't you remember me, Servant of the Lord Buddha? You bought me for gold pieces.

VASANTASENĀ I remember your face, sir, but I can't remember anything else about you. It seems I've been dead, and now I'm alive again.

SAṂVĀHAKA What happened, Servant of the Lord Buddha?

VASANTASENĀ What often happens to women of my profession. But somehow *I* survived.

SAṂVĀHAKA Now, get hold of this branch and see if you can stand up! [*She does so.*] There's a nunnery nearby, and I know one of the sisters in the Doctrine there! I'll take you there and you can rest a while and then go home. Now try to walk, Servant of the Lord Buddha. That's the way! Gently does it!

He who controls his hands, his mouth, his senses
he is a man in truth; the pomp and show
of palace and camp mean nothing to him, for
peace fills his heart, wherever he may go.

# Act IX

*Next day. The city administration headquarters. A court room. Enter usher.*

USHER They've told me to prepare the court for a sitting, and I'd better get busy because the judge'll be here any minute. [*Tidies court and arranges seats.*] Hullo! There's that low bastard the king's brother-in-law coming. I'd better make myself scarce. [*Exit.*]

[*Enter Saṃsthānaka, splendidly dressed.*]

SAṂSTHĀNAKA Now's my chance to finish off that wretch Cārudatta once and for all. I'll accuse him of killing Vasantasenā in the park. Hullo, no one here yet! I'll just sit down and wait till the judge comes [*does so*].

[*The usher re-enters and stands to attention by the door. Enter judge, with a lay magistrate (a local merchant), and the clerk of the court.*]

JUDGE

Remember, gentlemen, that hidden motives move
both plaintiff and defendant. Few men admit
their weaknesses and faults in court. The ruler
may well be ruined if his courts give false
judgments, and his judges incur censure.

And thus our task is hard. We must be well trained
in law, quick to detect deceit, well spoken,
not easily angered, alike to friend and foe,
showing no partiality to kinsmen,
reserving judgment till all the evidence
is heard. We must protect the weak and punish
the criminal. We must follow justice
wherein it leads us. We must be free from greed,
truthful, and fearless of the wrath of kings.

Usher! Announce the opening of the court!

*[Usher goes to the door of the court and shouts to the street outside.]*

USHER The court is in session! Let all who seek justice come in!

*[A number of citizens enter and take seats. When they have sat down the judge gives a sign to the usher.]*

USHER Let the first plaintiff come forward!

*[Saṃsthānaka quickly jumps to his feet, and advances to the judge's dais.]*

SAṂSTHĀNAKA I, a gentleman, a goodly human being, the brother-in-law of the king, wish to lodge a plaint.

JUDGE *[aside]* That madman Saṃsthānaka is looking very excited. It's said that red sky at sunrise presages the fall of a great man! There are many serious cases. I'll try to get rid of him. *[aloud]* Sir, we have very important business today. Please come back tomorrow.

SAṂSTHĀNAKA What, you won't hear my plaint? I tell you it's very serious. Moreover if you won't hear me I'll tell my sister's husband King Pālaka and I'll tell my sister and my mother too! Then he'll dismiss you and put another judge in your place.

JUDGE [*aside*] He seems very upset, and in that state he's capable of anything. Perhaps he has some really serious matter to lay before the court, and anyway he *was* first.
[*aloud*] Very well, sir, if your case is serious, we will hear you. Please sit down.

SAṂSTHĀNAKA [*aside*] Ha, he's changed his mind. That shows how scared he is of me. [*He sits down.*]

JUDGE Now make your deposition!

SAṂSTHĀNAKA I wish to make my deposition in private. I'll have you know I'm of an exceptionally illustrious family. In fact

my father is the father-in-law of the king
and the king is the son-in-law of my father.
I'm the brother-in-law of the king
and the king is my sister's husband!

JUDGE That is well known to me. Noble birth is quite irrelevant here—only virtue counts. Now, please declare your plaint.

SAṂSTHĀNAKA It is this. The husband of my sister, being pleased with me, gave me the best of the royal parks, the Puṣpakaraṇḍa Park, to amuse myself in. I visit it every day, to see that it is clean, tidy and well cared for. I have just seen there, by the will of fate, the dead body of a woman.

JUDGE And did you recognize that woman?

SAṂSTHĀNAKA Indeed I did, Your Honor. It was the beauty of the city, Vasantasenā. She had gone there wearing all her jewelry to meet one of her patrons and the brute strangled her to get her ornaments. I didn't do it!

JUDGE How useless the police are! Clerk! Note that he denies any complicity in the crime!

CLERK Yes, Your Honor.

SAṂSTHĀNAKA [*aside*] Oh dear, I nearly gave myself away!
[*aloud*] You heard me wrongly, Your Honor. I said I didn't see it—that is to say I didn't see the crime committed.

JUDGE Then how did you know that she was strangled to get her ornaments?

SAMSTHĀNAKA I knew she was strangled from the marks on her neck and I knew she'd been robbed because all her ornaments had gone.

MERCHANT Hm. Seems a fair answer.

SAMSTHĀNAKA *[aside]* Whew! That was a close call! I can breathe again.

JUDGE Usher! Call Vasantasenā's mother.

USHER Yes, Your Honor.

*[He goes out, and soon returns with the mother of Vasantasenā.]*

MOTHER Good morning, Your Honor.

JUDGE Please be seated! You are the mother of Vasantasenā?

MOTHER I am.

JUDGE Where is she at present?

MOTHER She's gone to a friend's house.

JUDGE What is his name?

MOTHER *[aside]* Oh dear, what a shameful thing to have to do! *[aloud]* I can't tell you, Your Honor, it would be a breach of my professional ethics.

JUDGE Don't be ashamed. Your ethics are not involved. By order of the court you *must* answer.

MERCHANT Yes, no harm will come to you if you speak the truth!

MOTHER Well, Your Honor, if you *must* know she went to a house in the Square of the Merchants which is the home of Cārudatta, the son of Sagaradatta and grandson of Vinayadatta. She's there now, putting her youth and beauty to a useful purpose, no doubt.

SAMSTHĀNAKA Did you hear that! Write it down! Cārudatta's the culprit.

MERCHANT I know Cārudatta. He can't be guilty of such a crime.

JUDGE Nevertheless, he must give an account of himself.

MERCHANT Quite so!

JUDGE Clerk, write down the deposition of the last witness. Usher, fetch Cārudatta, telling him politely that the court requests him to come, in order to answer a few questions.

[*Usher goes out. Returns with Cārudatta.*]

CĀRUDATTA [*aside*]

My left eye twitched, and on the road outside
a crow cawed hoarsely, and a venomous snake
glided across my path. These evil omens
perturb me. May heaven be my guard!*

[*aloud*] Good day, Your Honor. I believe you want to see me.

JUDGE [*aside*]

He's so well built, so open-eyed, so frank.
I can't believe he'd stoop to such a crime.
In elephants, horses, and cattle, as in men,
the face betrays the character, every time.

[*aloud*] Greetings, sir! Usher, give this gentleman a seat.

[*Usher does so. Cārudatta sits down.*]

SAṂSTHĀNAKA [*in a rage*] So we've got you, you murderer. A fine kind of justice this, to give a seat to a murderer like you!

JUDGE Master Cārudatta. I understand you are on intimate terms with this lady's daughter.

[*Cārudatta notices Vasantasenā's mother.*]

CĀRUDATTA [*surprised*] Why it's you, madam! Good day to you!

---

* Several verses have been compressed.

MOTHER Long life to you, my boy. That's Cārudatta. Such a nice young man for my daughter to have for a client.

JUDGE I understand, sir, that the courtesan Vasantasenā is your friend.

[*Cārudatta registers embarrassment.*]

SAṂSTHĀNAKA You can see from his shame and fright that he's hiding something. He killed her for her jewels, and there's no doubt about it.

JUDGE You are holding up the proceedings. Now you must give up all feelings of shame and speak the whole truth, by order of the court.

CĀRUDATTA Your Honor, who has laid a complaint against me?

SAṂSTHĀNAKA [*angrily*] I have!

CĀRUDATTA It will be a tough case if you are the accuser.

JUDGE Now, Master Cārudatta, will you admit that the courtesan is your friend?

CĀRUDATTA She is.

JUDGE And where is she now?

CĀRUDATTA She went home.

MERCHANT How did she go home? When did she go? Did anyone accompany her?

CĀRUDATTA [*aside*] How can I tell him everything? If I do I'll betray Āryaka, and I'll have confessed to aiding the king's enemies. [*aloud*] She went home. I've no more to say.

SAṂSTHĀNAKA [*raging*] You strangled her with your own hands in Puṣpakaraṇḍa Park so as to get her jewels! Now you say she went home, you liar.

CĀRUDATTA Oh! You're talking insanely.

JUDGE Would Master Cārudatta commit such a crime?

SAMSTHĀNAKA You're biased in his favor. The evidence will answer that question.

JUDGE Silence—you are insulting the king's justice! I repeat, I do not believe that a man like Cārudatta would commit such a crime.

MOTHER Your Honor, not long ago my daughter left her jewels in Cārudatta's care and they were stolen. Next day he gave her a very valuable pearl necklace in return. Of course he didn't do it. Oh my poor daughter, oh my poor daughter. [*Cries.*]

JUDGE Did she go on foot or in a carriage?

CĀRUDATTA I didn't see her, so I can't say.

[*Enter Vīraka, very angrily.*]

VĪRAKA Greetings, Your Honor.

JUDGE Ah Vīraka, the captain of the police. What brings you here?

VĪRAKA Sir, I have to report that while Candanaka and I were searching for Āryaka, after he escaped from prison, we came upon a covered carriage. Candanaka inspected it, and when I went to inspect it too he knocked me out and ran away.

JUDGE And do you know who was the owner of the carriage?

VĪRAKA The driver told us it was Cārudatta's and he was taking Vasantasenā to Puṣpakaraṇḍa Park.

SAMSTHĀNAKA Do you hear that, Your Honor?

JUDGE [*aside*]

The pure bright moon is veiled by an eclipse,
Dirt from the bank muddies the clean, still water.

[*aloud*] Vīraka, I'll look into your case later. Now will you please take a horse ride to Puṣpakaraṇḍa Park, and see if you can find the body of a woman.

VĪRAKA Yes, sir. [*Goes out and returns.*] Your Honor, I have to report that I found the body of a woman in the park but I couldn't identify it because the vultures and jackals had already eaten most of it.

MERCHANT How did you know it was a woman?

VĪRAKA From the hair and the remains of her clothing.

JUDGE [*aside*] How difficult this case is! The deeper I get into it the more complicated it becomes. I feel bogged down like a cow stuck in the mud!
[*aloud*] Master Cārudatta. I order you to speak the truth!

SAṂSTHĀNAKA I declare this court is biased in the prisoner's favor! He's obviously guilty and he's still allowed a seat.

JUDGE Usher, take away his seat.

[*Usher does so. Cārudatta sits on the ground.*]

CĀRUDATTA [*aside*] I sent Maitreya to Vasantasenā's house to give back the jewels she left in Rohasena's little clay cart. If only he'd come he could clear my name.

[*Enter Maitreya with the box of jewels concealed on his person.*]

MAITREYA [*to judge*] Your Honor, I was on my way to Vasantasenā's house when I heard that you had summoned my friend Cārudatta to the court.

JUDGE He is there.

MAITREYA Cārudatta, my dear friend! Why do you look so worried? What's the matter? Why did they summon you here?
[*to judge*] Your Honor, I ask permission to speak privately to Cārudatta.

JUDGE Permission is granted. [*They whisper together. Maitreya turns to the judge.*]

MAITREYA *[in the manner of a barrister]* Your Honor, our city of Ujjain is deeply indebted to this man who, in the time of his prosperity, endowed it with public buildings, monasteries, temples, parks, reservoirs, and wells. I ask you, is it conceivably possible that such a man could have committed so shocking a crime for a few cheap jewels? If, on the other hand, we turn to his accuser, we find a man of completely different stamp—I say it advisedly, though this Saṃsthānaka may be the brother-in-law of His Majesty the King—the son of an adulteress, an abandoned libertine, a man devoted to every kind of vice, and mentally defective—indeed an ape, wearing a fine robe and golden ornaments. I ask him in the presence of this court—does he really believe that Cārudatta is capable of so heinous a crime—a crime which will infallibly lead to destruction in this world and damnation in the next? *[His forensic manner has been wearing thin, and now completely disappears.]* You blasted son of a common procuress! Just you wait! You're as crooked as my staff here, and I'm going to break your head into a hundred pieces with it!

SAṂSTHĀNAKA Just listen, Your Honor, just listen! My accusation concerns Cārudatta, not this bald-headed Brahman, who threatens to break my head into a hundred pieces—this low son of a slave girl who calls himself a priest.

*[Maitreya brandishes his staff at Saṃsthānaka, who rises to his feet and strikes him. A scuffle follows, in the course of which the jewels which Maitreya is carrying fall to the ground.]*

JUDGE *[as they are fighting]* Order in Court. Usher, stop them at once!

SAṂSTHĀNAKA *[picking up the jewels]* Look, Your Honor! These are that poor woman's jewels. Ah! To think that she was murdered merely for these cheap trinkets.

MAITREYA Why don't you tell the truth, Cārudatta?

CĀRUDATTA The eyes of the king are weak, they miss the truth. Even though I deny it, still my fate is sealed.

JUDGE [*to Vasantasenā's mother*] Look carefully at this box of jewels, madam, and tell me whether you recognize it.

MERCHANT Now look very carefully, and tell us! Are you absolutely sure?

MOTHER Your Honor, I was deceived by the clever workmanship. It's not my daughter's.

JUDGE Now, madam, look at the jewelry, and tell me if you recognize it.

MOTHER I'd say that I've seen it before. I seem to remember a goldsmith making these ornaments for us.

CĀRUDATTA They belong to this lady's daughter, Your Honor.

MERCHANT How did they come into your possession?

Cārudatta, you must tell the whole truth.
The liar falls; who speaks the truth will rise
to heaven. So hide it not with lies!

Now, how did you really get this jewelry?

CĀRUDATTA Jewelry! Jewelry!! Always in trouble over jewelry! My little boy found them in his toy cart after Vasantasenā left. I assume she brought them.

SAṂSTHĀNAKA He's lying! He met her in the park and strangled her, and then he stole them.

JUDGE I must warn you, Master Cārudatta, you must speak the whole truth. How is it if Vasantasenā left her jewels with your son, that she was later strangled in Puṣpakaraṇḍa Park? You must know that, though I do not want to be compelled to take such measures, it is in my power to have you whipped.

CĀRUDATTA [*aside*]

My family is a righteous one, and I
have always striven to do right. But now
I am accused of a crime most vile and mean!

Let them have their way! Without Vasantasenā
life is worth nothing to me. Though I die
with reputation fouled, my heart is clean!

[*aloud*] It is said, Your Honor, that

I am a brutal criminal
with no thought of the world to come,
and further that the beautiful Vasantasenā—

SAṂSTHĀNAKA —was killed by your hands! Go on, admit it! Tell them that you killed her!

CĀRUDATTA You have spoken for me.

SAṂSTHĀNAKA You hear, Your Honor, you hear! He killed her, and now there can't be any doubt about it! I demand that he be arrested and executed.

JUDGE The prince is right! Guards! Arrest Cārudatta.

[*The guards do so.*]

MOTHER Oh please, please Your Honor. If my daughter's killed she's dead and nothing can be done about it. I can't really believe he's done it, though he seems to have admitted it. I want him to live. Please don't condemn him Your Honor, I'm the one who's been wronged, not him, and I don't want to lodge a complaint. Please let him go!

SAṂSTHĀNAKA Get out, you old bag! It's nothing to do with you.

JUDGE Madam, you must go. Guards, see this old lady out!

MOTHER [*weeping*] My boy! My dear boy! [*Exit.*]

SAṂSTHĀNAKA [*aside*] Now I've achieved something that's really worthy of me! I'll be off. [*Exit.*]

JUDGE Master Cārudatta, it is I who give judgment, but the punishment is decided by the king. Usher, go to His Majesty, King Pālaka, and report the matter, taking the clerk's notes of the case. Clerk of the Court! Add a note to the effect that according to the Code of Manu a

Brahman should not suffer imprisonment or corporal or capital punishment, and the highest penalty that can legitimately be inflicted is exile.

*[The clerk does so. Usher takes his notes, exits and returns almost immediately, with a document.]*

USHER *[reading]* "His Majesty King Pālaka commands that, inasmuch as Cārudatta has murdered Vasantasenā for the sake of her jewelry, of trifling value, that same jewelry shall be hung around his neck and he shall be led round the city in chains, to the beat of the drum, and shall be taken to the southern cemetery, where he shall be executed. And whosoever in future shall commit a similar crime shall suffer the same penalty, with public humiliation and painful death!"

CĀRUDATTA The king shows no mercy! How many thousands of innocent people have suffered death at the hands of unjust kings? Maitreya, my friend! Go and bid my wife farewell for me, and look after my little Rohasena, my only son.

MAITREYA Oh, how can I protect a tree cut off at the root?

CĀRUDATTA No, no, it is not like that. The dead live on in their sons. Love him, just as you loved me.

MAITREYA We've been such good friends for so long, I don't think I want to go on living without you.

CĀRUDATTA You must, Rohasena needs you.

JUDGE *[pointing at Maitreya]* Usher, send that fellow away.

*[Usher does so.]*

JUDGE Now remove the prisoner, and make preparations for the execution.

USHER *[to Cārudatta, politely]* You must come with me, sir.

CĀRUDATTA King Pālaka,

you are killing me, a priest,
through the word of an evil man, my enemy.
I pity you, for you and all your line
will suffer far greater agony of mind and body
in the depths of hell, than I shall know today.

All right, I'm ready.

[*Exeunt.*]

# Act X

*The same day. The city of Ujjain from the central square to the south gate. Enter two untouchables who are the public executioners, leading Cārudatta, wearing red garments, Vasantasenā's jewelry hung round his neck, and a garland of oleanders.*

FIRST EXECUTIONER: Make way, good people! Make way for Cārudatta!

CĀRUDATTA:
My face is wet with my own bitter tears
My limbs are weary and covered with dust and grime,
I wear a wreath of funeral oleander
Already the carrion crows call rancorously
as though they smell the blood of the sacrifice.

SECOND EXECUTIONER: Come, Cārudatta! Make way, good people! Make way!
Why do you look on, as though at a festival,
while a just man is cut down by the axe of death.
Remember this man, who rose like a mighty tree,
whose branches once gave shelter to many birds.

CĀRUDATTA: How strange the tricks of fate that
I should thus be dragged along,
my body smeared with paste of blood-red sandal,
I, a living man,
led like a beast prepared for sacrifice.

VOICES IN THE CROWD* Shame! Down with the bloody king and his judges! Let him go! He's sure to go to heaven! [*Many of the crowd show signs of deep emotion and are in tears.*]

FIRST** EXECUTIONER
Through the will of fate, this noble citizen
is falsely accused, and led away to die.
Surely the very air weeps at the sight
and lightning falls from an unclouded sky.

SECOND EXECUTIONER
See how the heavens are darkening, how the clouds
cry like a throng of women, looking down
upon this man being led to death, and with them
the people weep. See, on the busy highway
the dust is laid by rain and human tears.

FIRST EXECUTIONER This is the square, where we must make the proclamation! [*Beats a drum.*]

SECOND EXECUTIONER Attention! Attention! Here stands Master Cārudatta, the son of Sagaradatta and grandson of Vinayadatta the merchant. The courtesan Vasantasenā was lured by this criminal to Puṣpakaraṇḍa Park, and there murdered by strangling for the sake of her jewelry. The jewelry was found in his possession and he admits the crime. Therefore His Majesty King Pālaka has decreed that he be put to death. Should any man in future commit such a crime His Majesty King Pālaka decrees he shall suffer the same punishment.

ROHASENA'S VOICE Daddy! Daddy!!

MAITREYA'S VOICE [*off stage*] My friend! My dear old friend!!

FIRST EXECUTIONER Clear the way, citizens, so that Master Cārudatta can see his son! Right! Come along, little boy, come along!

---

* This is based on Cārudatta's verse 6.

** In the original this and the following verse are apparently spoken by the two executioners.

*[Enter Maitreya and Rohasena.]*

ROHASENA Daddy! My dear daddy!

MAITREYA Oh my dear old friend—shall I ever see you again?

CĀRUDATTA My son! Maitreya!

I shall long so thirst in the world to come,
for small will be the offerings made by these tiny hands.

What can I give my son? Yes, this sacred cord is still mine—the badge of the Brahman, more precious than pearls or gold.

*[Removes his sacred cord and gives it to Rohasena.]*

ROHASENA Where are you taking my father?

CĀRUDATTA My child,

round my neck a wreath of oleander,
a burden of bitter grief in my heart,
I go today to my own execution,
like a goat to the priest who slays him at the altar.

ROHASENA Why are you going to kill my father?

FIRST EXECUTIONER It's the king's orders. We're not to blame.

ROHASENA Kill me, and let my father go!

FIRST EXECUTIONER *[almost in tears]* Little boy, God bless you for saying that!

CĀRUDATTA *[embracing Rohasena and smiling through his tears]*

Oh love's a treasure rich and poor may own,
more soothing to the heart than any salve.

MAITREYA I say, you two! You seem good-natured fellows. Won't you execute me in his place and let him go?

CĀRUDATTA *[courageously]* Heaven forbid! Oh, how wrong I was when I used to complain

that a poor man's friends all deserted him!
Behind every window half-hidden faces watch me,
calling my name, and sobbing with compassion.

FIRST EXECUTIONER Make way there! Make way!
Why do you stand and gape, while a just man
with no hope for his life suffers like this,
such deep humiliation, like a golden bowl
that slowly sinks in a deep muddy well?

[*They move on, and halt outside Saṃsthānaka's mansion, where Sthāvaraka, in chains, looks from an upper window.*]

STHĀVARAKA What! They're going to execute Cārudatta, when I know he's innocent. And I'm up here in prison and can't help. [*Shouting at the top of his voice.*] Listen everybody! He didn't do it! I took her to the park in my carriage by mistake, and my master strangled her because she wouldn't love him! [*normal voice*] Oh dear, I'm too far away! They can't hear me! There's only one thing I can do to save him! Better I'm killed, than Cārudatta. If I die I'll go to heaven. [*He leaps out of the window, and slowly picks himself up.*] Thank God I'm all right. And my chains are broken in the fall. I'll run after them . . . [*shouting*] Hi! Executioners! Stop! Stop!!

FIRST EXECUTIONER Listen, someone's calling us. [*They pause and wait.*]

STHĀVARAKA Stop! He didn't do it. She got into my carriage by mistake and I took her to the park. It was my Master Saṃsthānaka who strangled her, because he was madly in love with her and she wouldn't take any notice of him!

CĀRUDATTA Who can this be who, in my deepest need,
comes like a rain cloud to the drought-parched corn?

FIRST EXECUTIONER Is what you say really true?

STHĀVARAKA I swear it! He had me put in chains and locked in an upper room for fear I might give him away!

*[Enter Saṃsthānaka.]*

SAṂSTHĀNAKA *[rubbing his stomach]* What a splendid meal—meat flavored with sharp tamarind, fish soup, and vegetables, finished off with rice pudding and treacle! *[listening]* A lot of noise out there! I wonder if it's Cārudatta being led to his execution? I'll have a look! It's said that if a man watches his enemy being killed he'll never suffer from eye trouble in his next birth. I'll go up to the tower and watch . . . I say, what a lot of people have turned out to see him. It's not fair for a poor miserable wretch like him! It's as though a really great man like me were being executed! *[nervously]* What! Sthāvaraka's gone! He must have jumped out of the window, chains and all. Supposing he's let the cat out of the bag. I'd better find him.

*[Goes down and chases after the procession.]*

STHĀVARAKA *[looking back]* Here he comes, masters.

FIRST EXECUTIONER

Out of the way, good people, close your doors and
stay quiet. A mad bull rushes upon us and his
horns are sharpened by evil.

SAṂSTHĀNAKA Hi! Hi there! Make way! Sthāvaraka, my dear man, come with me. Get away from this crowd!

STHĀVARAKA You low swine! You're not satisfied with murdering Vasantasenā. You've made up your mind to kill Cārudatta as well!

SAṂSTHĀNAKA *[nervously]* I didn't do it. A rich aristocrat like me would never think of killing a defenseless woman.

CROWD He did it! He did it! Cārudatta's innocent!

SAṂSTHĀNAKA *[aside]* Damn and blast them all! Why didn't I kill Sthāvaraka too, while I was about it? That's what comes of magnanimity! *[aloud]* It's not true, gentlemen, it's not true! I caught this man stealing my gold and so beat him and shut him up. He hates me, and so he's telling lies about me.

*[Secretly offers Sthāvaraka a bracelet, aside.]* Sthāvaraka, my boy! Take this and tell them you were lying.

STHĀVARAKA *[taking bracelet and showing it to crowd]* Look, look gentlemen. He's trying to bribe me!

SAṂSTHĀNAKA *[snatching back the bracelet]* Why! This is the very bracelet he stole from me! If you don't believe me look at the marks on his back!

FIRST EXECUTIONER *[looking]* He's right. We can't accept his evidence.

STHĀVARAKA Nobody believes the word of a slave! Master Cārudatta, there's nothing more I can do! *[Falls at Cārudatta's feet.]*

CĀRUDATTA

Get up, my helper in need, the unexpected
defender of those in trouble, righteous friend.
You risked your life to save me, like a hero.
You can do no more! Fate triumphs in the end.

SAṂSTHĀNAKA Why are you taking so long about it? Kill him right now.

FIRST EXECUTIONER We were to kill him in the cremation ground. If you're in such a hurry you'd better kill him yourself.

ROHASENA Please, you men, kill me, and let my father go!

SAṂSTHĀNAKA I order you to kill the two of them.

CĀRUDATTA That madman is capable of anything. My son, you'd better go back to Mommy now!

MAITREYA How can I live without you, my dear old friend!

CĀRUDATTA You're a free man, Maitreya, and it's not right that you should think of killing yourself. Take Rohasena back to his mother!

*[Maitreya and Rohasena fall at Cārudatta's feet, weeping.]*

SAṂSTHĀNAKA Don't let that boy go! I said he was to be killed along with his father.

[*Cārudatta registers fear.*]

FIRST EXECUTIONER: The king's orders said nothing about killing the child. We've no authority to do so. Now off you go, little boy! Off you go!

[*Exeunt Maitreya and Rohasena.*]

[*The procession reaches the burning ground.*]

FIRST EXECUTIONER: We must wait while I write the inscription to put on the body.
[*aside to Second Executioner*] You know, my old father, who was the royal executioner before me, and who's now gone to heaven, always used to tell me that if I ever stepped into his shoes I ought to delay executions as long as I possibly could.

SECOND EXECUTIONER: Oh, why was that?

FIRST EXECUTIONER: You see, it's just possible that at the last minute someone will bribe the king to let the prisoner go; or the queen may give birth to a son and the king may decide to reprieve all the prisoners condemned to death to celebrate the occasion; or an elephant may go mad and break his chains and come charging down on the burning ground, and so give the prisoner a chance to escape in the confusion; or there might even be a revolution and the new king might set all the prisoners free.

SAṂSTHĀNAKA: [*alarmed*] Did I hear you say "revolution"?

FIRST EXECUTIONER: Quiet! Don't disturb us. We're busy writing the inscription.

[*Saṃsthānaka, holding Sthāvaraka tightly by the arm, stands at a distance.*]

FIRST EXECUTIONER: Master Cārudatta! Please understand that it's by the king's orders that we have to do this, and not by our own will.

The sun and moon in heaven from time to time suffer misfortune, and mortal men cannot escape it. He who rises must fall, and he who falls will sooner or later rise. Dying is really only like changing your clothes. Take courage, master.

CĀRUDATTA

I have been wronged by the word of powerful
and wicked men, and by the will of fate.
Yet somehow righteousness may yet prevail.
Somehow I know, whether reborn on earth
or in the heavens, Vasantasenā will
restore my tarnished and dishonored name.

FIRST EXECUTIONER

[*to Second Executioner*] Well, we can't delay the job much longer, I'm afraid! [*to Cārudatta*] Now, sir, you must get ready. Don't be afraid! It will be all over very quickly! Lie down sir, and don't move. One blow, and you'll be in heaven!

CĀRUDATTA

Very well! [*Does as instructed.*]

FIRST EXECUTIONER

[*Draws sword. Raises it, and then lowers it, pausing to say a prayer.*] Mother of all things, Blessed Lady who dwelled in the forests and whose home is in the high mountains, have mercy upon Cārudatta, have mercy on us all. Thou who most lovest the base and lowly folk among whom we were born, I pray thee to save this man at the last, and in thy great power set him free, that the people of the untouchables may forever sing thy praises.

[*Enter Vasantasenā, followed at a distance by Saṃvāhaka. Her appearance is tense, wild, and majestic, as though driven by some superhuman power. The executioner throws away the sword, gazing at her with intense awe.*]

FIRST EXECUTIONER

A miracle! The goddess has come! She has answered my prayer!

VASANTASENĀ

Stop! Stop! You're killing him for murdering me, and I'm still alive.

SECOND EXECUTIONER: The goddess has come in the form of Vasantasenā herself, to save a righteous man from death.

SAṂVĀHAKA: Praise be to the Lord Buddha that we were just in time! I was taking Vasantasenā home when we heard the noise of a crowd over here, and came to see what was the matter. We just heard the end of the proclamation.

FIRST EXECUTIONER: We must report this matter to the king right away!

*[The two executioners start moving off.]*

SAṂSTHĀNAKA: *[terrified]* It's unbelievable! The damned bitch! She's come to life again! This is no place for me! I'm off! *[Runs away.]*

FIRST EXECUTIONER: Remember our orders—execute the man who strangled her. After him! *[They chase Saṃsthānaka.]*

CĀRUDATTA:

Is this another Vasantasenā, or may it be
a goddess come to save me at my call?
Or am I now in heaven, rewarded for
the wrongs I suffered by reunion
with her I loved so well? Or, possibly
Vasantasenā was not dead at all!

VASANTASENĀ: *[weeping]* Yes, Cārudatta. It's Vasantasenā, the wretched woman for whose sake you suffered so much!

CĀRUDATTA: *[embracing her]* My darling. You really are alive!

There is no need to bathe with streaming tears
your breasts, for you have brought me back to life!
How great the power of love, to wake the dead!
This funeral robe and garland shall become
the bridegroom's festal dress, and the grim drum
the ceremonial music for our wedding.

VOICES OFF STAGE: Long live Āryaka! Long live King Āryaka! *[Enter Śarvilaka in splendid military uniform with guards.]*

ŚARVILAKA: *[sees Cārudatta, joyfully]* How good to find you alive, Master Cārudatta! I was afraid I'd be too late. As soon as I heard you were to be executed I came at once. [*to guard*] Go back and report this to the king at once.

CĀRUDATTA But who are you sir?

ŚARVILAKA Don't you remember the thief who robbed your home, and took the jewels left in trust with you? I am that sinner, and I'm at your mercy!

CĀRUDATTA Friend, don't say such things. What you did was for my good, in the long run! [*Embraces him.*]

ŚARVILAKA What's more, Āryaka has killed that wicked King Pālaka. You remember Āryaka—the man you saved by giving him your carriage?

CĀRUDATTA Yes, I remember! That was after you'd helped him escape from prison. I'm very glad.

ŚARVILAKA And in gratitude for your help he's sent me to tell you that you are appointed viceroy of the city of Kuśāvatī.

[*Enter Executioners, leading Saṃsthānaka, his hands bound behind him.*]

FIRST EXECUTIONER Come on there, you cur. You're not the king's brother-in-law any longer. It's time you got the treatment you deserve!

SAṂSTHĀNAKA [*aside*] It seems it's all up with my brother-in-law, so it's all up with me too. Nobody will help me now! [*Sees Cārudatta.*] I don't know, he's supposed to be the help of the helpless. There's no harm in trying. [*aloud*] Noble Lord Cārudatta, save me, save me! [*Falls at Cārudatta's feet.*]

ŚARVILAKA [*angrily*] Drag him off. Don't let him pollute Lord Cārudatta. Now sir, what would you like us to do with him? Shall we have him pulled to pieces on the rack, or eaten alive by dogs, or impaled, or sawn in half? What do you suggest?

CĀRUDATTA Will you do whatever I tell you?

ŚARVILAKA Of course!

SAṂSTHĀNAKA Lord Cārudatta! I'm under your protection. Save me, I won't do it again!

VOICES IN CROWD Kill him, kill him!

*[Vasantasenā takes the funeral garland from Cārudatta's neck and places it on Saṃsthānaka.]*

SAṂSTHĀNAKA Have pity on me! I promise I won't kill anyone again! Save me! Save me!

CĀRUDATTA
When your old enemy, however wicked,
seeks your protection, falling at your feet,
you should not put him to the sword or hang him—

ŚARVILAKA —but have him eaten up by ravenous dogs!

CĀRUDATTA No! Strike him only by your acts of kindness.

ŚARVILAKA That's a nice idea! But what do you want us to do with him?

CĀRUDATTA Set him free!

ŚARVILAKA *[rather surprised and disappointed]* Well—if you say so, that's what we'll do!

SAṂSTHĀNAKA *[as the Executioners untie his hands, quite calmly]* Would you believe it? I'm still alive! *[Exit with Executioners.]*

*[Enter Maitreya, Rohasena, Dhūtā and Radanikā.]*

ROHASENA *[running]* Daddy, Daddy! He's still alive!

*[Cārudatta picks him up and hugs him.]*

DHŪTĀ My dear husband! I almost put an end to my own life!

MAITREYA It's really wonderful! I never thought I'd see my old friend again. We heard about the revolution and hurried here in the hope that you'd still be alive! The truth always wins through in the end!

CĀRUDATTA Come, Maitreya! [*Embraces him.*]

DHŪTĀ [*seeing Vasantasenā*] And my dear sister's safe and sound too! [*Embraces her.*]

VASANTASENĀ Now I'm happy and safe at last!

RADANIKĀ My dear master. How strange is fate. [*Falls at his feet.*]

CĀRUDATTA Get up, Radanikā my dear! [*Helps her up.*]

[*Enter guard, with written message for Śarvilaka.*]

ŚARVILAKA Lady Vasantasenā! His Majesty is most impressed by what he has heard of your nobility of soul and loyalty and he orders that you are released from all bonds and contracts incurred in the course of your former profession, and are thus free to become Cārudatta's lawful wife.

VASANTASENĀ Sir, I'm deeply in His Majesty's debt for this favor.

[*Śarvilaka places a veil over Vasantasenā's head as a mark of her new status.*]

ŚARVILAKA [*to Cārudatta*] And what can we do now to reward this reverend monk?

CĀRUDATTA Your Reverence—what would you most like?

SAṂVĀHAKA More than ever I am aware that nothing is stable, nothing endures. And more than ever, I am drawn to the life of religion. I want nothing at all!

CĀRUDATTA He won't change his mind, but he's so sincere and pious, he could well be made chief abbot of all the Buddhist monasteries in the country, if he'd accept that post.

SAṂVĀHAKA [*without enthusiasm*] I accept. Praise be to the Lord Buddha.

ŚARVILAKA And what about yourself? What more can we do for you?

CĀRUDATTA I can't think of anything I want at all!

For now my innocence is proved at last.
The foe who fell at my feet has been set free.
My good friend Āryaka has now uprooted
his enemies, and rules the land as king.
And I have won my love, and you, dear friend
Maitreya, are beside me once again!
What else remains, that I should now desire it?
Oh, mortal men are like the many buckets
which in an endless chain rise from a well.
Some destiny makes full, and some it empties,
some are raised high, and some fall very low,
and some are shaken, and some dashed together.

So, my friends, let this be the final benediction.
Now may the cows yield us their richest milk,
and may the earth be carpeted with corn.
May the rain fall at the appointed time,
and the winds blow gently, refreshing all men's hearts.
May all the priests and monks be saints of virtue,
and righteous kings, their foes subdued, rule gloriously,
and all things born know happiness forever!

# *Appendix I. The Author*

## I

The authorship of the Sanskrit play, translated into English by A. L. Basham, has been attributed to Śūdraka. This attribution naturally arouses one's curiosity: who was Śūdraka?

Unfortunately, "Śūdraka's identity and authorship must yet be regarded as unsolved problems."[1] One cannot hope to solve these problems with the available evidence, which is largely mythical and anecdotal in character; "to melt down the legends and recoin historical truth from them, when they bear upon their very face the stamp of myth, is possible but not convincing."[2] Nevertheless, the material is worth examining. It may not yield the satisfaction of a conclusion, but understanding why a conclusion is elusive may itself be a source of some satisfaction.

As to the problem of Śūdraka, "we know nothing beyond what has been said in the prelude" to the play;[3] this prologue is presented below. After the benediction with which Sanskrit plays begin, the director enters and announces:

> No more of this tiresome waste of time that'll only wear thin our audience's curiosity! I prostrate myself before you gentlemen and beg to announce to you that we have decided to stage a Fantasy for you, which is entitled *The Little Clay Cart*. The poet, of course, was a king whose steps had the poise of an elephant, whose eyes the light of a cakora bird's, whose face the beauty of the full moon, King Śūdraka, stalwart leader of the twiceborn, celebrated poet, profound man of character! Indeed, he was a scholar of the Veda of the Hymns and the Veda of the Chants, mathematician, arbiter of elegances, and

> trainer of elephants. Darkness was lifted from his eyes by the grace of Śiva; and when he had seen his son established as king and offered with great magnificence a Horse Sacrifice, he entered, at the age of one hundred years and ten days, the sacred fire. Śūdraka was addicted to battle, but without imprudence. He was a paragon of theologians as well as a great ascetic, a king of the world, it has been said, eager to wrestle with enemy elephants.
>
> In this play of his you will meet
>
> One poor young merchant from Ujjayinī,
> A Gentleman, whose name is Cārudatta;
> And, lovely as the Spring, a Courtesan,
> Vasantasenā, who is in love with him:
>
> King Śūdraka has shown here how their love
> Provokes against them a conspiracy,
> How justice is perverted, and how crooks
> Conduct themselves, and Destiny disposes.[4]

The purpose of a prologue is to provide information about the author to the audience. But in this case that information seems to involve some misinformation, and perhaps even disinformation[5]—a point noted by J. A. B. van Buitenen at the very outset: "An ancient Indian play, it was said, is traditionally signed with the name of its author in the prologue. The director of the play appears before the audience and announces its title and the name of its author, so that no confusion can arise. But as luck will have it, in *The Little Clay Cart* there is considerable confusion."[6]

What are the sources of this confusion? In the prologue the author describes his own death.[7] This is unusual, to say the least. The fact, however, does not seem to faze traditional commentators by whom Śūdraka's "announcement of his own death is ascribed to the author's prophetic foresight, the result of astrological computation."[8] Modern scholars take a more realistic view:

> Scholars have spent considerable effort on identifying the King Śūdraka to whom the play is attributed in the Prologue. But at least part of the Prologue must be by a later hand, since it is said that Śūdraka died at the age of one hundred years and ten days; and however many accomplishments are ascribed

to him, he could hardly have written his own obituary. As King Śūdraka was a legendary figure in narrative literature, the probabilities are that a *later* tradition linked him with the author of the play. It has been argued convincingly that such a linkage could have been forged only if the author's name was in fact Śūdraka. The name is not at all uncommon.[9]

Two points, however, need to be borne in mind in this context: (1) The posthumous postscript referred to above raises several possibilities that have not escaped the notice of scholars, though opinion is sharply divided as to its implication. Kāshīnāth Pāṇḍurang Parab, the most economical in drawing his conclusion, holds that the verses giving an account of the playwright's own death "are from another pen."[10] J. A. B. van Buitenen suggests that the name Śūdraka might be a pseudonym adopted by the author of the play: "it means 'little Śūdra or servant' and might even have been adopted as a sobriquet or pseudonym."[11] The scholar explains:

> At the beginning of this century manuscripts were discovered which purported to contain the plays of a Bhāsa who had long been known as a playwright, since Kālidāsa mentioned him with respect in the prologue to one of his own plays. Controversy has raged ever since as to whether these are indeed Bhāsa's plays or later fabrications. The question is of interest to us since these Bhāsa plays include a fragmentary play called *Cārudatta*. On perusal this play, of which we have four acts, proves to be the basis of *The Little Clay Cart*.[12]

Van Buitenen offers his own speculation as to the play's authorship:

> Śūdraka himself found Bhāsa's play incomplete, whether the author had left it that way or chance had destroyed the latter part; and . . . he set out to write the completion of it. The name Śūdraka might then well be a modest gesture showing his indebtedness to Bhāsa from "the little servant." If this conjecture is correct, it also suggests an explanation of the name of the play. Titles of plays ought to show at least the name of one of the heroes, if not both; the other word in the title should indicate a crucial element in the play: *Śakuntalā and the Ring, The Minister's Seal, Yaugandharāyaṇa and His Promise, Vāsavadattā*

> *in the Dream*, etc. The little clay cart figuring in the title hardly figures in the play; if it be true that Vasantasenā's jewels contained in the *Cart* seem to indict Cārudatta for her murder, the point is that Cārudatta is not finally executed and that what saves him are Vasantasenā's timely appearance and Āryaka's palace revolution. But the choice of the title makes nice sense if once more the intention is modest; compared with Bhāsa's chariot, Śūdraka's play is just a fragile little cart of clay.[13]

The name could also be a pseudonym in another sense. It has been suggested that "as royal authors in historic times were not averse to having works written for themselves, it has been maintained by those who believe in an historical Śūdraka that the real author, like a wise and grateful courtier, ascribed his work to his royal patron and allowed his own name to perish."[14]

All the suggestions, though ingenious, lack proof. However, the curiosity of post-mortem penmanship should not provoke us to throw out the baby with the bath water. For one thing, "the prelude is found substantially in the drama Daridra-Cārudatta"[15] attributed to Bhāsa; for another, although "the use of the perfect tense, indicative of an event long past, in stanzas 3, 4, and 7 of the prologue is significant," "it need not imply that the information is not based upon tradition, or is not trustworthy."[16] As Sushilkumar De observes:

> In spite of the number of legends which have gathered round the name of Śūdraka, its reputed author, nothing is known of him beyond the somewhat fanciful account given in a Prologue of the play. We are told in this eulogistic reference that the author was a great Brahman king of the name of Śūdraka; and among the curious details of his excellences, we find that he was proficient in the Ṛgveda and the Sāmaveda, in mathematics, in the art concerning the courtesan and in the lore of elephants,—*statements which it is not impossible to support, to a limited extent, from the knowledge betrayed in the drama itself.*[17]

Moreover, the name Śūdraka itself is somewhat curious, considering the fact that in the eulogy he is described as "chief among the *dvijas*," or twice-borns. The *Śūdras* are denied that status.[18] As if being a *śūdra* is not modest enough, humility being the prize virtue of that *varṇa*,[19] the name Śūdraka carries the additional diminutive suffix,[20] adding a further touch of humility. These considerations have led to the suggestion that Śūdraka was a low-born king.

> It is not improbable that there was a rājā, who bore the epithet Śūdraka, on account of being of lowly origin, and had adopted the drama of Bhāsa afresh. In this drama we find revolution heralding in matters relating to manners and customs, and in it a case of removal of a legitimate king by a cowherd has been described; besides we find predilection of Prākrit dialects in it and not for straight standard Sanskrit and notice certain deviations from the strict rules of dramaturgy, and lastly strong Buddhist spirit is permeating it—all this appears to go to point out that the author of the Mṛcchakaṭika does not belong to any of the two highest Brāhmanical castes.[21]

The suggestion, though interesting, is not without its difficulties. The fact that Pāṇini refers to the *Brahmasūtra* as the *Bhikṣusūtra* seems to indicate that Hindu and Buddhist semantic fields sometimes overlapped.[22] There are suggestions in the Pali canon itself that seem to attribute a monk's lack of understanding to his low birth.[23] More pertinently, the author of our work is fully aware of Brahmanical prejudices against the *śūdra* and the tone of their expression also seems Brahmanical. The most relevant and interesting passage in this connection is from Act IX, verse 21: *vedārthān prākṛtas tvam vadasi na ca te jihvā nipatitā*.[24] "You dare recite the Veda and your tongue does not shrivel and fall out?"[25] In this translation by van Buitenen the word *prākṛta* remains untranslated. A. W. Ryder renders it as "illiterate."[26] The line evokes all the imprecations found in the *Manusmṛti* for the *śūdra* who dares to recite a Vedic text.[27]

We are thus left with two alternatives: Śūdraka was either a very modest king or a king from a very modest background.

The play contains explicit references to Buddhism. It is important to emphasize that these references are not stereotypical. They are not references to a straw-figure Buddhism, the kind one might find in literature as a stock-in-trade. The Buddhism represented here replicates real life. A stereotypical portrayal, in fact, would militate against the realistic spirit of the entire play itself. "The accurate mention of the Buddha rites and the flourishing condition of Buddhism, indicated by the recommendation or appointment of one of the dramatis-personae as the chief of the Vihāras or Buddhistic monasteries, speak of a day evidently different from those of other dramas employing the mendicants of this religion as mere pīṭhamardadakas or pīṭhamarddikās, i.e. panders."[28]

Apart from explicit references, it has even been claimed that the play contains implicit references to Buddhism. Henry W. Wells argues that

> even the name of Śūdraka's play points to religious connotations. The "toy cart" is presumably a reference to the celebrated Buddhist parable of the burning house. In this parable the house signifies the material world and the worldly life of man. The most effective means that the gods have found to lure man out of his predicament is a subterfuge. Reason is of small avail. But on being told the toy carts are just outside his door, the wise man, at least, leaves his fatal dwelling to play with these deceptive trifles. They are no trifles but lures to catch the soul.[29]

Indu Shekhar sees the general social conditions associated with Buddhism as providing the social background of the play, though indirectly. He remarks that "the main features of the problem relating to [the play's] authorship and the social background . . . indicate beyond doubt that *Śūdraka's* antecedents are dubious, and that he purposely selected a theme exalting a non-Aryan regime over a tyrant Brāhmanical royalty."[30] Shekhar concludes his discussion of the play[31] by arguing that, "strange though it may appear, it is a hard fact that the first dramatist of Sanskrit literature was a Buddhist [Aśvaghoṣa], and a close second hails, as far as can be seen, from a non-Aryan stock of whom so little is known." The argument has its limitations, as not much is known of many Sanskrit dramatists and their work has been assigned "to periods ranging from the second century B.C. to the sixth century A.D."[32] But it also possesses enough force to raise the following question: Does this mean that Śūdraka was a Buddhist?[33] The fact that the benediction is addressed to Śiva makes this unlikely.[34] However, it has already been pointed out that one "familiar with the moral teachings of Buddhism will not miss to see in this drama clear traces of the moral teachings of Buddhism." Therefore one might conclude that the "poet Śūdraka appears to have been a liberal Hindu with strong Buddhist leanings."[35] Although Śūdraka was himself not a Buddhist king, he does seem to be aware of how kings dealt with Buddhism. "It is remarkable that the new king Āryaka, at the end of the drama, makes the monk the head of the cloister." This indicates an awareness on the part of the author that "the right of selecting the head of Buddhist monasteries was exercised by the rulers."[36]

We may surmise from the foregoing discussion that the author of the play was probably a king with a somewhat unusual though not unpopular[37] name who as a Hindu harbored Buddhist sympathies. What more can be gleaned from the evidence before us? For instance, have we any indication of the part of the country the author may have hailed from?

The popular indigenous accounts associated with Śūdraka locate his origins in southern India.[38] Scholars are inclined to agree. K. P. Kulkarni is willing to acknowledge that Śūdraka appears "familiar with the south though the style he has used in the play is the Pāñchālī style,"[39] as he "mentions the Sahya mountain, the Karṇāṭakalaha and also some mleccha tribes in southern India."[40] Shekhar is willing further to agree that R.D. Karmarkar "has convincingly proved that Śūdraka was a southerner." As Shekhar writes,

> In act X of the play, the goddess Durgā is extolled as *sahyavāsinī* which is typical of a southerner. In the North this goddess is popular as *vindhyavāsinī*. Śūdraka refers to *Karṇāṭa, Draviḍa* and *Cola* and also uses some expressions intimately associated with the South. The fact that Śūdraka was a southerner is further confirmed by the extensive researches made by Saletore who treats the author as an historical figure identifying him with Śivamara I who ruled between A.D. 675 to 725. According to Saletore Candanaka's speech using the phrase "*Karṇāṭa-kalaha-prayoga*" smacks of the aggressive nature of the Kannadigas. Besides, the geographical references made by Śūdraka also point to the author's bias for the South. The names Kuśāvatī and Venā are the names of two rivers in the Deccan. The term *kāṇelīmātaḥ* seems to refer to some old family with Kāṇelī as a variation of *kaṇṇahaḷḷi*, the term "*mātaḥ*" corresponding to a popular suffix form of "*ammā*," commonly used in the South. The names Śūdraka and Cārudatta have been quite popular in the history of the Deccan. The merchant princes have very

often been compared to Cārudatta. All these references convincingly show that the author belonged to the South, where dance and drama traditions were deep-rooted."[41]

## II

What then do we know about the author, if we do not choose to ignore the issue altogether?[42] It does not seem unreasonable to conclude that the author of the play was a king (as he is never referred to as other than a king)[43] by the name of Śūdraka (as the play is ascribed to none else)[44] who was somewhat partial to Buddhism, hailed from south India, and probably flourished around the fourth century.[45]

Given the abundance of discussion on the question, our conclusion is remarkably scanty. Yet the fact that we know so little about the author may not after all be such a bad thing. A. W. Ryder's thoughts on the matter offer consolation:

> Our very lack of information may prove, to some extent at least, a disguised blessing. For our ignorance of external fact compels a closer study of the text, if we would find out what manner of man it was who wrote the play. And the case of King Shūdraka is by no means unique in India; in regard to every great Sanskrit writer,—so bare is Sanskrit literature of biography,—we are forced to concentrate attention on the man as he reveals himself in his works.[46]

We must then move on, in the same spirit, from the author to his work.

# *Appendix II. The Play*

## THE TYPE OF PLAY

The Hindus have been accused of having so strong a passion for classification that in the Kāmasūtra one virtually ends up with a classification of passion itself. Such a comment may not be inappropriate in introducing a play that has been described as "not a love-story but a story of love."[47]

To place the present play in its proper context, one might first observe that

> Sanskrit drama proliferated into many types. Bharata mentions ten main varieties known in his time. The typology is generally clear, but, in a few cases, rather blurred. The generic term of the drama is Rupaka. Among its various forms, the highest is the Nataka. The heroic or erotic Nataka, usually consisting of five to ten acts, is given a legendary theme and a hero of elevated rank. The Prakarana is also a full-fledged form, but it is a comedy of manners of a rank below royalty, with an invented plot and characters drawn from the middle class or even lower social grades. Thus the main division seems to be between the heroic drama and the social play.[48]

In terms of this division *The Little Clay Cart* is a social play, technically known as a *prakaraṇa,* a species of *rūpaka* or drama.[49] The characteristic features of a *prakaraṇa* are thus described in Hindu dramaturgy:

> In Prakaraṇa, the event should be a pure fiction drawn from real life and Śṛṅgāra, the permanent sentiment. The hero may be a Brāhmaṇa, or a minister, or a merchant, and should be brave and calm, and longing for worldly enjoyments; the

> heroine may be a girl of high family or a courtesan. Because of the threefold heroes and heroines it is of three kinds.

In the present case the hero, Cārudatta, is a Brahman; the heroine, Vasantasenā, starts out as a courtesan but ends up as the wife of Cārudatta. The famous dramaturgical text, the *Daśarūpaka*, cites the *Mṛcchakaṭika* as an example of a *prakaraṇa*, where the heroine is both courtesan and highborn lady (*kulajā*),[50] hence the play belongs to the *saṅkīrṇa* subclass. "The example of the *Mṛcchakaṭikā* induced few imitations, doubtless because would-be imitators had the sense to realize the appalling difficulties of producing anything worthy of setting beside such a masterpiece."[51]

## HISTORICAL ANTECEDENTS

Parts of the *Mṛcchakaṭika* display a striking resemblance to the fragments of another Sanskrit drama, *Daridracārudatta*, ascribed to Bhāsa. The exact nature of the relationship between the two is again a matter of considerable complexity and controversy,[52] but most scholars seem to favor the view that the *Mṛcchakaṭika* is "a genial, elaborate and later adaption, perhaps a continuation of Bhāsa's Daridracārudatta."[53]

From our point of view as readers rather than as critics, interest lies in the fact that while the plot of the *Mṛcchakaṭika* involves a love story allied to a dynastic revolution, this political dimension is absent in *Daridracārudatta* as it's known to us. "The political background which permeates the entire drama, even from its prologue, in which there is a reference to King Pālaka, is entirely absent in the *Cārudatta*."[54]

## DATE OF THE PLAY

The date of the play is a thorny issue.[55] We shall satisfy ourselves here by first determining its *terminus ad quem* and then by indicating its most likely date.

The first mention one finds of Śūdraka—and it is indicative of his high reputation[56]—is in the *Kāvyālaṅkārasūtravṛtti*[57] of Vāmana. Thus, it is "not possible to assign a very late date to the *Mṛcchakaṭika*. Vāmana already in the 8th century refers (iii.2.4) to a composition by Śūdraka, and also quotes two passages anonymously, one of which also occurs in the *Cārudatta*, but the other does not."[58] It is true that the *Mṛcchakaṭika* is not mentioned by name, but given that hardly any other work *by* Śūdraka is mentioned,[59] as distinguished from several *about* him, we stand on firm ground.

On the likely date of the play there is considerable difference of opinion. The present trend seems to be to assign it to the Gupta period, with some scholars opting for a time before, some after, and some during that period. Earlier dates have also been suggested.

Those who wish to assign it to a period just prior to the Guptas argue as follows: As was noted earlier, the first four acts of this ten-act play follow closely the four acts of the play *Cārudatta* ascribed to Bhāsa, a play which in all probability Śūdraka decided to carry to completion—a circumstance not unknown in the history of Sanskrit literature. Kālidāsa refers both to Bhāsa as his predecessor and also to a narrative about Śūdraka composed by Rāmila and Saumilla. These indications seem to make Śūdraka "Kālidāsa's approximate contemporary,"[60] as A. L. Basham puts it.

Two other pieces of evidence serve to strengthen this conclusion: The text of the play quotes Manu as an authority regarding the inviolability of the person of a Brahman, the caste (*varṇa*) of the hero Cārudatta (IX.39), and the *Manusmṛti* is now usually assigned at the latest to the second century A.D. A curious piece of astrological lore also assists in placing Śūdraka in the classical age of the Guptas (circa A.D. 300-600). In Hindu astrology, planets, like human beings, can like, dislike, or be indifferent to one another. Though classical Hindu astrology views Jupiter and Mars as friends, the play refers to them as enemies (IX.33), betraying an earlier view which was superseded once the later one was adopted in an authoritative treatise on the subject by Varāhamihira, who belongs to the sixth century A.D.[61] According to this view, then, one would not be too wide off the mark in placing Śūdraka towards the beginning of the Gupta period.[62]

Other scholars prefer to assign the author and the play to the Gupta period itself. James Roose-Evans, for instance, declares that the play "was written in the fifth century, and this period marked the most brilliant of Sanskrit drama. Thus the drama of India reached its height in a period commonly regarded as the most brilliant in Indian culture."[63] Some scholars would prefer to place it in the post-Gupta period. A curious piece of evidence, ingenious if not entirely convincing, has been presented in this case by Adya Rangacharya (formerly known as R. V. Jagirdar), who speculates:

> Is it possible that the play was written somewhere between the fall of the Gupta Empire and the rise of King Harṣa? Could we, for example, read such a meaning in the fourth verse of Act VIII where the Viṭa describes the park as follows—
>
> aśaraṇa-śaraṇa-pramoda-bhūtaiḥ
> vana-tarubhiḥ kriyamāṇa-cāru-karma,
> hṛdayam iva durātmānam *a-guptam*
> navam iva rājyam anirjitopabhogyam. (68)
>
> "Here the trees are doing a good deal by joyfully offering shelter to the homeless; the park (however) is like the untutored (i.e. uncultured) heart to the wicked; it is like a new kingdom the titleship (upabhogya) to which is not yet proved." In the above, we can understand a pun on the word "a-gupta" and the meaning as, "It is like the heart of the wicked; it is like a kingdom where the Guptas are no more and the new kings have not established their authority." Further we may note that Āryaka who is successful in the revolution is called a gopāla-dāraka.[64]

The issue is a difficult one. "The opinions expressed and the dates ascribed are so divergent," according to Indu Shekhar, "that one could easily form an independent treatise if discussed in detail."[65] Even then one cannot be certain that the enterprise will yield a firm conclusion. A scholar of such high caliber as A. B. Keith seems to throw up his hands in despair after surveying the evidence: "We are left, therefore, with no more than impressions, and these are quite insufficient to assign any dates to the clever hand which recast the *Cārudatta* and made one of the great plays of Indian drama."[66]

However, scholarship, like nature, abhors a vacuum and there is an increasing tendency to place Śūdraka about A.D. 400 or a little earlier,[67] as suggested by A. L. Basham.

## TRANSLATIONS OF THE PLAY

The play has been translated into several European languages.[68] The following list is confined to the major English translations as providing the backdrop for A. L. Basham's.

(1) 1826: Horace Hayman Wilson translates it for the first time into English under the title: *The Mrichchakati or The Toy Cart, A Drama Translated from the Original Sanskrit.*[69]

(2) 1905: Arthur William Ryder's translation of the *Mṛcchakaṭika* appears as Volume 9 in the Harvard Oriental Series. It is based on the edition of Parab and the metrical components of the play are translated in verse.[70]

(3) 1938: Revilo Pendleton Oliver's translation appears as Volume 35 of the *University of Illinois Bulletin* (No. 78, May 27, 1938).[71]

(4) 1965: James Roose-Evans adapts it for the stage in Volume 29 of *Plays of the Year* (1964-1965),[72] with the editor of the series J. C. Trewin expressing the hope that "one day somebody will describe the vicissitudes of the famous Sanskrit drama on the English stage."[73]

(5) 1968: Translation by J. A. B. van Buitenen appears from the Columbia University Press as one of the two plays in his *Two Plays of Ancient India.* Some metrical components are translated in verse while others are rendered in prose.

To illustrate differences in nuance in the various translations of the *Mṛcchakaṭika*, several renderings of the same verse are here presented. The verse selected is No. 16 of Act V. This verse tries to capture the eagerness of the courtesan Vasantasenā as she goes to meet her lover Cārudatta at the onset of the rainy season:

> meghā varṣantu garjantu
> muñcantv aśanim eva vā
> gaṇayanti na śītoṣṇam
> ramaṇābhimukhāḥ striyaḥ

(1) Horace Hayman Wilson (1826):

> Let the clouds fall in torrents, thunder roar,
> And heaven's red bolt dash fiery to the ground,
> The dauntless damsel, faithful love inspires,
> Treads boldly on, nor dreads the maddening storm.[74]

(2) Arthur William Ryder (1905):

The clouds may rain, may thunder ne'er so bold,
May flash the lightning from the sky above;
That woman little recks of heat or cold,
Who journeys to her love.[75]

(3) A. Berriedale Keith (1924):

Let the clouds rain, thunder,
or cast down the levin bolt;
women who speed to their
loved ones reckon nothing of
heat or cold.[76]

(4) Revilo Peddleton Oliver (1938):

Though the rain descend, though
the clouds resound, though the
thunderbolt be hurled down, women
are not deterred by heat or
by cold when they go to
rejoin the one whom they love.[77]

(5) James Roose-Evans (1965):

Though the rain descend, though
the clouds resound, though
the thunderbolt be hurled
down, we are not to be
deterred by heat or cold
when we go to rejoin our beloved.[78]

(6) J. A. B. van Buitenen (1968):

Let clouds hurl thunderbolt, or rain, or growl,
A woman yearning for her love counts fair nor foul![79]

(7) A. L. Basham (1968):

Though the rain pour, though the clouds roar
though thunderbolts fall from above her,
a woman cares nothing for heat or cold
when she goes to meet her lover!

*Appendix II*

# GENERAL COMMENTS

Happily, more can be said about the play than about its author or its date. Its predominant mood is characterized by the sentiment of nobility or magnanimity. Cārudatta, the hero, seems to incarnate the loftiest verses of the *nītiśataka* of Bhartṛhari. He seems to salvage nobility out of every situation. If the thief makes away with the jewelry deposited with him on trust, he is happy that the thief did not go empty-handed. If now he has to make good the lost jewelry, his wife, not to be outdone in nobility, offers her own; and the comment he makes to his wife even manages to show some traces of feminism: "a woman through wealth becomes as powerful as a man." To himself he offers the consolation that he is not poor, for he has a wife whose value, in biblical metaphor, exceeds that of rubies. A wife in need is a wife indeed. While Cārudatta carries on with the courtesan, the wife is self-effacing to the point of almost not appearing in the play. The two women—courtesan and wife—vie with each other not to be outdone in nobility and embrace as sisters when they meet. Even Cārudatta's son, once whimpering over the clay cart that gives the play its title, is in the end willing to be executed in his father's stead despite his tender age, a gesture which melts the hearts of the executioners. Cārudatta's friend, Maitreya, perceiving that there is no good greater than that a man lay down his life for his friend, is equally willing to die in his place, but civil law, unlike the transferability of karma, does not allow for substitutionary atonement. It is striking that Maitreya is purportedly the *vidūṣaka,* a role in Sanskrit plays that serves little more than to offer comic relief, display an addiction to gluttony, and follow the ups and downs of the hero's love life. Although Maitreya does take "keen interest in delicious food," "his steadfastness to his friend in times of adversity and warmth of his heart distinguish him from his fellow-characters in Sanskrit drama."[80]

Vasantasenā, the heroine of the play, is a courtesan but is "a hetaira who hated her position, and whose great aim was to be recognized a woman of family (*kulastrī*), and thus be permitted legitimate marriage in lieu of compulsory polyandry"[81]—a noble goal which she does achieve in the end. Madanikā, the maidservant, becomes a free woman and is thus also ennobled; and Saṃvāhaka, a former masseur and gambler, turns a new leaf and becomes a Buddhist monk—a conversion in which he is only further confirmed at the end of the play by the vicissitudes he witnesses and is sometimes a party to. Even the judge in the courtroom scene insists on the impartiality of justice, while, ironically, a miscarriage of justice is occurring. Even the two outcastes who are the executioners, in a verse they address to Cārudatta's son, do not fail to remind the audience that virtue is the true test of caste: "Boy, we aren't pariahs, although we are born from a pariah family. The real, the evil pariahs are those who do violence to a decent man" (X.22, van Buitenen's translation). The verse echoes the sentiments expressed in the *Mahābhārata* (12, 182.4-8). Cārudatta at one point demands of the pariahs a "Brahman's gift." They are shocked: "What? You demand a Brahman's gift from the likes of *us*?" Nobility, like pollution, spreads.

The play's themes vary from the humorous to the virtuous; the same sacred cord connects them. In one scene a Brahman uses the sacred cord in lieu of a measuring tape while committing a felony; in another Cārudatta offers his own sacred cord to his son as a final memento just before Cārudatta's impending execution. Both humor and pathos seem bound by the same cord. Even the villain, who by definition cannot be a virtuous person, is made into the object example of virtuous conduct: Cārudatta, who acquires power of life and death over him when it is discovered that the villain has perjured himself, forgives him, choosing to smite him by wielding virtue as a weapon.

Ultimately, of course, underlying all this nobility is a profound humanity, an ethic that would place the duty[82] of being a conscientious human being (*sādhāraṇa dharma*) above that of a robotic conformity to the duties of one's class and stages of life (*varṇāśrama dharma*). The *Law's of Manu* set it out: "Abstention from injuring [creatures], veracity, abstention from unlawfully appropriating [the goods of others], purity, and control of the organs, Manu has declared to be the summary of the law for the four castes."[83]

It seems to me that it was this human quality of the play which so attracted Professor Basham to it, and attracted him sufficiently to undertake the literary enterprise of translating it into English for the benefit of a grateful posterity. For Professor Basham, "the most striking feature of ancient Indian civilization [was] its humanity."[84] Perhaps the same can be said of this play in which Indian society in all its variety is so vividly represented.

*Appendix II*

# NOTES

1. Sushilkumar De, *History of Sanskrit Literature* (University of Calcutta, 1947), 241.
2. De, *History of Sanskrit Literature*, 241.
3. M. Winternitz, *History of Indian Literature*, trans. Subhadra Jha (Delhi: Motilal Banarsidass, 1963), vol. III, part I, 224.
4. J. A. B. van Buitenen, *Two Plays of Ancient India* (New York: Columbia University Press, 1968), 52-53. Although the translation here is in prose, the piece in which the author signs himself in the original text is in verse.
5. The particulars of the prologue are accepted somewhat uncritically, it would appear, by H. R. Aggarwal, *A Short History of Sanskrit Literature* (Delhi: Munshi Ram Manohar Lal, 1963), 194.
6. van Buitenen, *Two Plays of Ancient India*, 30.
7. This point has naturally exercised the minds of scholars. C. Kunhan Raja encapsulates the problem well:

   > In Sanskrit dramas there is generally a prologue in which some information about the poet and the drama is given. In this drama, the author is spoken of as a great king with learning, who performed the famous *Aśvamedha* Sacrifice which is performed by all sovereign kings with imperial sway and who died after living for a little over a hundred years. Certainly this information about the author could not have been given by the author himself. Either the drama is not by Śūdraka; the poet wrote it and gave it out as the work of the great scholar king Śūdraka. Or it may also be that Śūdraka wrote it and that the prologue was added later. The latter is not a plausible alternative. In the former alternative we are depriving the drama of a really worthy authorship.

   In the end "All that we can say is that according to tradition Śūdraka was a king and a scholar and a poet and that the drama *Mṛcchakaṭika* is known as a work of Śūdraka; the difficulty arises since, in the prologue to the drama, the poet is mentioned as dead. Is the whole drama by another poet or is the prologue added later? Both suppositions create problems." (*Survey of Sanskrit Literature* [Bombay: Bharatiya Vidya Bhavan, 1962], 163-64.)
8. Kāshīnāth Pāṇḍurang Parab, ed., *The Mṛichchhakaṭika of Śūdraka with the commentary of Pṛithavīdhara* (Bombay: Nirṇaya Sāgar Press, 1902), 3.
9. van Buitenen, *Two Plays of Ancient India*, 30.
10. Parab, *Mṛichchhakaṭika*, 3.

11. van Buitenen, *Two Plays of Ancient India*, 30.

12. van Buitenen, *Two Plays of Ancient India*, 30.

13. van Buitenen, *Two Plays of Ancient India*, 31-32. From this point of view it is noteworthy that "Śūdraka defies the convention of naming after the names of the hero and the heroine, as we have it in Bhavabhūti's Prakaraṇa, the *Mālatīmādhava*" (De, *History of Sanskrit Literature*, 244, note 1). *The Little Clay Cart* technically falls in the category of *prakaraṇa*.

14. This possibility is mentioned though not supported by De, *History of Sanskrit Literature*, 241. Arthur A. Macdonell, however, thought that although it is "attributed to a king named Śūdraka, who is panegyrised in the prologue, it is probably the work of a poet patronised by him, perhaps Daṇḍin, as Professor Pischel thinks" (Arthur A. Macdonell, *A History of Sanskrit Literature* [New York: Haskell House Publishers, 1968, 1900], 361).

15. Winternitz, *History of Indian Literature*, 225.

16. De, *History of Sanskrit Literature*, 240, note 2.

17. De, *History of Sanskrit Literature*, 240. Emphasis added. An earlier editor of the play, Kāshīnāth Pāṇḍurang Parab, however, is less inclined to trust the information provided (*Mṛichchhakaṭika*, 1):

> The autobiographical account, inserted in the play, informs us that Śūdraka, the regal bard, was the author of the [Mricchakatika]. The authenticity of such statements is sometimes invalidated by the literary forgeries at times brought to light. Suspicion as to their genuineness is especially roused because of the occasional attribution of literary works to kings or dignitaries with a view to advantage and also because sovereigns, particularly the warlike, are less prone to such undertakings. Accordingly the prologue of our play is generally discredited.

Krishna Chaitanya also seems similarly inclined. He notes that Śūdraka is "a legendary king referred to in later literature and some scholars think that the playwright remained anonymous and attributed the work to the king to gain prestige for the work" (*A New History of Sanskrit Literature* [London: Asia Publishing House, 1962], 307).

Indu Shekhar is even more forcefully negative:

> Though references to the legendary name of Śūdraka are very numerous, no convincing proofs of his antiquity are yet available. Curiously enough he styles himself *dvija-mukhyatamaḥ* which runs counter to reason, because no highborn person, much less a learned king, would allow himself to be addressed as Śūdraka, a diminutive amongst the low-born. That not much reliance can

> be placed on the authenticity of the prologue is further confirmed by another claim averring that Śūdraka entered the fire having performed the horse sacrifice at the age of a hundred years and ten days. This indicates that the prologue was added at a later date and can in no way be regarded authentic.

(*Sanskrit Drama: Its Origin and Decline* [Leiden: E. J. Brill, 1960], 115-16.)

18. A. L. Basham, *The Wonder That Was India* (New York: Grove Press, 1954), 138, 143, 161-62.
19. Basham, *The Wonder That Was India*, 138.
20. See P. K. Gode and C. G. Karve, Eds. in chief, *V. S. Apte's The Practical Sanskrit English Dictionary* (Poona: Prasad Prakashan, 1957), vol. I, 514.
21. Winternitz, *History of Indian Literature*, 225-26.
22. Pāṇini (4.3.110).
23. A. L. Basham, "Theravāda Buddhism," in Wm Theodore de Bary, ed., *Sources of Indian Tradition* (New York: Columbia University Press, 1958), 103, note 1.
24. Parab, *Mṛichchhakaṭika*, 242.
25. van Buitenen, *Two Plays of Ancient India*, 158-59.
26. Arthur William Ryder, trans., *The Little Clay Cart* (Cambridge, Mass.: Harvard University Press, 1905), 143.
27. Ram Sharan Sharma, *Śūdras in Ancient India* (Delhi: Motilal Banarsidass, 1958), 120.
28. Parab, *Mṛichchhakaṭika*, vii-viii.
29. Henry W. Wells, *The Classical Drama of India* (London: Asia Publishing House, 1963), 159. The point seems a bit forced. The reference apparently is to an account in the Lotus Sūtra.
30. Shekhar, *Sanskrit Drama*, 115.
31. The following scenario is developed by Indu Shekhar as constituting the societal context of the play.

> Manu says that a child born of a Brāhmaṇa *ambaṣṭha* from a (Śūdrā) mother, is Ābhīra. All the above evidence indicates that the Ābhīras were regarded a low class. Intercourse between the wandering tribes of Ābhīras and their most civilised Aryan neighbours must have upset the priestly class. It is possible that lured by the physical charms of Ābhīra girls, the Aryan youth endangered the sanctity of the Aryan race and thus may have incurred the displeasure of the priests. Kṛṣṇa and Gopāla legends,

believed to have been added later, support this admixture of races. By showing preference for this community of the low born, Śūdraka exhibited his own bias in no smaller degree.

Furthermore,

> Whatever be the date and the achievements of the play, the fact remains that Śūdraka could never have been a Kṣatriya or a Brāhmaṇa king as depicted in the prologue of the play. Instead of showing any leanings towards the Brāhmanical priesthood, he supported the plebeians in their upheaval and introduced a large number of characters drawn from the lower order of society, which otherwise were ignored by more famous dramatists. Not content with these deviations, he exalted the role of a courtesan raising her to the status of a lady. Vasantasenā, a dancing girl of Ujjayinī, emerges a noble, pious and devoted woman to her love. Perhaps she could never attain this status if she were to marry a character of equal rank. Though such cases of love were neither rare nor shocking, yet none showed enough boldness to make them the theme of a play or a poem. Possibly the theme reflects a period when the injunctions of the Law-givers were not effective.

(*Sanskrit Drama*, 120).

32. De, *History of Sanskrit Literature*, 240.

33. The suggestion is sometimes implied, rarely made. Adya Rangacharya, however, speculates, considering the fact that a menial is converted to Buddhism in the play, that a character of a higher status would have converted to Buddhism in the play, if the author had himself been a Buddhist (*Drama in Sanskrit Literature* [Bombay: Popular Prakashan, 1967], 120).

34. Winternitz, *History of Indian Literature*, 232, note 3.

35. Winternitz, *History of Indian Literature*, 232.

36. Winternitz, *History of Indian Literature*, 232, note 2.

37. See, for example, Aggarwal, *Short History of Sanskrit Literature*, 193-94; De, *History of Sanskrit Literature*, 241.

38. M. Krishnamachariar, *History of Classical Sanskrit Literature* (Madras: Tirumalai-Tirupati Devasthanams Press, 1937), 572.

39. K. P. Kulkarni, *Drama and Dramatists* (Satara: K. P. Kulkarni, 1927), 100.

40. Kulkarni, *Drama and Dramatists*, 101.

41. Indu Shekhar, *Sanskrit Drama*, 118. The references are to "R. D. Karmarkar,

Proceedings of Oriental Conference, Trivandrum 1937; his article in New Indian Ant. II (1939-40), 76-85; His *Mṛcchakaṭika*, Poona (1937), pp. VIII-IX."

42. Henry W. Wells displays a charming and disarming indifference toward the whole issue:

> Although for actual performance the play's authorship is clearly of small importance, there is a possible aesthetic significance in the readiest answer to this question. My answer is simply and in all seriousness that which Lord Byron gave facetiously to the mystery of "Junius," namely, that the person in question "was nobody at all"! It will be recalled that the king Śūdraka is described as having "the dignity of an elephant, the eye of a *chakora*, a face like the full moon, and a body harmoniously proportioned. The profundity of his wisdom was unfathomable. He knew the *Rig Veda*, the *Sāma-Veda*, mathematics, the science of erotics, and the art of training elephants. By the grace of Śiva, the veil of ignorance was lifted from Śūdraka's eyes, so that, after he had witnessed the coronation of his son and had performed the incomparable horse-Sacrifice, he, having attained the incomparable age of one hundred years and ten days, cast himself into the flames." There is much more to the same effect. The Manager, who utters these words, speaks humorously of his own harangue. Scholarship has failed to fix upon any king who can with any degree of confidence answer this description. Have we here the flattery of an ancestor of a patron? Or is "Śūdraka", perhaps, as much a fiction as any character in the play, a dream-idealization, a humorous wish-fulfilment, of the author's own psyche? A writer capable of creating as many convincing characters as appear in this play could assuredly create an imaginary author with the greatest of ease. The superlatives, even for Sanskrit literature, read very like parody, and the play itself is singularly well stocked with parody. Until better evidence than now available is procured, the present writer prefers to regard "Śūdraka" himself as a charming fictional creation and a cypher as mystifying as Byron's interpretation of "Junius".

(*Classical Drama of India*, 165).

43. See, for example, Kulkarni, *Drama and Dramatists*, 97.

44. Pischel suggested that the play may have been authored by Daṇḍin, but the suggestion has found little favor. See, for example, Parab, *Mṛichchhakaṭika*, ii-iv; Winternitz, *History of Indian Literature*, 226, note 2.

45. The date of Śūdraka is hard to determine. As Sylvan Lévi put it: "The name Śūdraka is as familiar to literature as it is strange to literary history" (see Parab, *Drama and Dramatists*, i). The question of the date of the play and hence of the author is discussed in the next section.

46. Ryder, *Little Clay Cart*, xv.

47. Rangacharya, *Drama in Sanskrit Literature*, 125.

48. Chaitanya, *New History of Sanskrit Literature*, 287.

49. Parab, *Mṛichchhakaṭika*, 2. The play, however, does not fit the category neatly. As Sushilkumar De notes (*History of Sanskrit Literature*, 244, note 1): "It is noteworthy that Śūdraka defies the convention of naming his play after the names of the hero and the heroine, as we have it in Bhavabhūti's Prakaraṇa, the *Mālatīmādhava*. In contravention of dramaturgic prescription, Cārudatta does not appear at all in acts ii, iv, vi and viii; while his simple-minded and whole-hearted friend, Maitreya, with his doglike faithfulness, does not conform to the technical definition and has none of the grosser traits of the typical Vidūṣaka. The presence of shady characters is, obviously, not entirely legitimate, for this makes the author of the *Daśarūpaka* call it a Saṃkīrṇa Prakaraṇa . . . inasmuch as such characters as apparently appropriate to the Bhāṇa or Prahasana."

50. D. R. Mankad, *The Types of Sanskrit Drama* (Karachi: Urmi Prakashan Mandir, 1936), 52; also see H. H. Wilson et al., *The Theatre of the Hindus* (Calcutta: Sushil Gupta [India] Limited, 1955), 52.

51. A. Berriedale Keith, *The Sanskrit Drama in Its Origin, Development, Theory and Practice* (Oxford: Clarendon Press, 1924), 257.

52. Winternitz, *History of Indian Literature*, 223, note 1, 228, notes 1 and 2; De, *History of Sanskrit Literature*, 242, note 1; Krishnamachariar, *History of Classical Sanskrit Literature*, 575, note 2.

53. Winternitz, *History of Indian Literature*, 224. See also Krishna Chaitanya, *New History of Sanskrit Literature*, 307: "The play is expanded from the fragments of Bhāsa's *Charudatta*. Only one writer has suggested that *Charudatta* is derived from *Mriccha Katika*. The majority of critics are of the opinion that the indebtedness runs the other way. But the *Mriccha Katika* is in ten acts while the *Charudatta* fragment consists only of four acts and the reshaping is brilliant enough to merit evaluation as an original."

54. De, *History of Sanskrit Literature*, 245, note 1.

55. See Winternitz, *History of Indian Literature*, 225, note 2; Chaitanya, *New History of Sanskrit Literature*, 307.

56. Parab, *Mṛichchhakaṭika*, ii.

57. This text is cited as *Kāvyālaṅkāravṛtti* by Winternitz, *History of Indian Literature,* 225, note 2.

58. De, *History of Sanskrit Literature,* 242.

59. A *bhāṇa,* however, is ascribed to him (De, *History of Sanskrit Literature,* 242, note 4). Could it be that the present play itself attracts that category? (See De, 244, note 1.)

60. Basham, *The Wonder That Was India,* 441.

61. It is possible, however, that "this stanza may have been taken from Bhāsa" (R. P. Oliver, *The Little Clay Cart* [Urbana: University of Illinois Press, 1938], 26, note 42).

62. Basham, *The Wonder That Was India,* 441; van Buitenen, *Two Plays of Ancient India,* 32:

> It is generally agreed that the *Cart* is one of the earlier plays of Sanskrit literature, and prior to Kālidāsa. Certain resemblances to *The Minister's Seal*—the dilapidated garden, the execution scene, etc.—make it likely that it is close in time to Viśākhadatta's play (the reign of Candra Gupta II Vikramāditya); one is likely to have borrowed from the other, and, given Śūdraka's more ancient style of Prakrits and far looser adherence to the dramatic conventions, he was the earlier writer and Viśākhadatta was the borrower.

63. James Roose-Evans, "The Little Clay Cart: A Note," in J. C. Trewin, ed., *Plays of the Year* (London: Elek Books, 1965), vol. 29, 22.

64. Rangacharya, *Drama in Sanskrit Literature,* 121.

65. Shekhar, *Sanskrit Drama,* 115.

66. Keith, *Sanskrit Drama in Its Origin,* 131.

67. See, for example, G. K. Bhat, *Preface to the Mrcchakatika* (Ahmedabad: New Order Book Co., 1953), chapter X; Oliver, *Little Clay Cart,* 26.

68. De, *History of Sanskrit Literature,* 239.

69. Horace Hayman Wilson, trans., *The Mrichchakati or The Toy Cart* (Calcutta: U. Holcroft, Asiatic Press, 1826).

70. Arthur William Ryder, trans., *The Little Clay Cart* (Cambridge, Mass.: Harvard University Press, 1905).

71. Oliver, *Little Clay Cart.*

72. J. C. Trewin, ed., *Plays of the Year* (London: Elek Books, 1965) vol. 29, 22-116.

73. Trewin, *Plays of the Year,* 9.

74. Wilson, *The Toy Cart*, 108.
75. Ryder, *Little Clay Cart*, 82.
76. Keith, *Sanskrit Drama in Its Origin*, 139.
77. Oliver, *Little Clay Cart*, 125.
78. Trewin, *Plays of the Year*, 71.
79. van Buitenen, *Two Plays of Ancient India*, 112.
80. M. A. Mehendale, "Language and Literature," in R. C. Majumdar, ed., *The Age of Imperial Unity* (Bombay: Bharatiya Vidya Bhavan, 1968), 265.
81. A. B. Keith, *A History of Sanskrit Literature* (Oxford University Press, 1920), 271.
82. *Manusmṛti* X.63.
83. G. Bühler, trans., *The Laws of Manu* (Delhi: Motilal Baṇarsidass, 1964; first published by Oxford University Press, 1886), 416.
84. Basham, *The Wonder That Was India*, 9.

# *Select Bibliography*


Aggarwal, H. R. *A Short History of Sanskrit Literature.* Delhi: Munshiram Manoharlal, 1963.

Bhat, G. K. *Preface to the Mrcchakatika.* Ahmedabad: New Order Book Co., 1953.

Basham, A. L. *The Wonder That Was India.* New York: Grove Press, 1954.

Bühler, G., trans. *The Laws of Manu.* Delhi: Motilal Banarsidass, 1964, 1886.

Chaitanya, Krishna. *A New History of Sanskrit Literature.* London: Asia Publishing House, 1962.

De, Sushilkumar. *History of Sanskrit Literature.* Calcutta: University of Calcutta Press, 1947.

de Bary, Wm Theodore, ed. *Sources of Indian Tradition.* New York: Columbia University Press, 1958.

Devasthali, G. V. *Introduction to the Study of Mrcchakatika.* Poona: Oriental Book House, 1951.

Godabole, N. B. *Toy Cart.* Bombay: Government Central Press [Bombay Sanskrit and Prakrit Series, no. 52], 1896.

Gode, P. K., and C. G. Karve, eds. *V. S. Apte's The Practical Sanskrit English Dictionary.* Poona: Prasad Prakashan, 1957.

Goswami, Mahaprabhulaha et al., eds. *Mrcchakatikam.* Benares: Chowkhamba Sanskrit Series Office [Haridas Sanskrit Granthamala, 252], 1954.

Kale, M. R., ed. and trans. *The Mrichchhakatika of Sudraka.* Delhi: Motilal Banarsidass, 1972, 1924.

Keith, A. B. *A History of Sanskrit Literature.* Oxford: Oxford University Press, 1920.

———. *The Sanskrit Drama in Its Origin, Development, Theory and Practice.* Oxford: Clarendon Press, 1924.

Krishnamachariar, M. *History of Classical Sansrit Literature.* Delhi: Motilal Banarsidass, 1970, 1937.

Kulkarni, K. P. *Drama and Dramatists.* Satara: K. P. Kulkarni, 1927.

Kunhan Raja, C. *Survey of Sanskrit Literature.* Bombay: Bharatiya Vidya Bhavan, 1962.

Lal, P. *Great Sanskrit Plays.* Norfolk, Conn.: New Direction Books, 1957.

Macdonell, Arthur A. *A History of Sanskrit Literature.* Delhi: Motilal Banarsidass, 1965, 1900.
Mankad, D. R. *The Types of Sanskrit Drama.* Karachi: Urmi Prakashan Mandir, 1936.
R. C. Majumdar, ed., *The Age of Imperial Unity.* Bombay: Bharatiya Vidya Bhavan, 1968.
Misra, J. V. *Mrchhakatikam.* Benaras: Caukhamba Surabharati Prakasana [Caukhamba Surabharati Granthamala, 76], 1985.
Neurarkar, V. R., ed. and trans., *The Mrichchhakatika.* Bombay: Bombay Book Depot, 1937.
Oliver, R. P., trans., *Mrcchakatika—The Little Clay Cart: A Drama in Ten Acts, Attributed to King Śūdraka.* Westport, CT: Greenwood Press, 1975, 1938.
Parab, Kāshīnāth Pāṇḍurang, ed. *The Mṛichchhakaṭika of Śūdraka with the commentary of Pṛithavīdhara.* Bombay: Nirṇaya Sāgar Press, 1902.
Rangacharya, Adya. *Drama in Sanskrit Literature.* Bombay: Popular Prakashan, 1967.
Ryder, A. W., trans. *Mṛcchakaṭika—The Little Clay Cart.* Cambridge, Mass.: Harvard University Press, 1905.
Sharma, Ram Sharan. *Śūdras in Ancient India.* Delhi: Motilal Banarsidass, 1958.
Shekhar, Indu. *Sanskrit Drama: Its Origin and Decline.* Leiden: E. J. Brill, 1960.
Śūdraka, *The Mrichchhakati (microform): A Comedy: with a commentary explanatory of Pr[a]akrit Passages.* Calcutta: Education Press, 1829.
Trewin, J. C., ed. *Plays of the Year.* London: Elek Books, 1965.
van Buitenen, J. A. B., trans. *Two Plays of Ancient India.* New York: Columbia University Press, 1968.
Wells, H. W. *The Classical Drama of India.* London: Asia Publishing House, 1963.
———, trans. *Classical Triptych: Sakuntala, The Little Clay Cart, Nagananda, A New Rendering in English Verse.* Mysore: University of Mysore, 1970.
Wilson, Horace Hayman. *The Mrichchakati or The Toy Cart.* Calcutta: U. Holcroft, Asiatic Press, 1826.
———. et al. *The Theatre of the Hindus.* Calcutta: Sushil Gupta [India] Limited, 1955.
Winternitz, M. *History of Indian Literature.* Translated by Subhadra Jha. Delhi: Motilal Banarsidass, 1963.

# *Index*